Additional Exercises for

# Successful College Writing

Additional Exercises for

# Successful College Writing

**Fifth Edition**

**SKILLS · STRATEGIES · LEARNING STYLES**

**Carolyn Lengel**

HUNTER COLLEGE

**Jess Carroll**

MONTANA STATE UNIVERSITY IN BOZEMAN

**BEDFORD/ST. MARTIN'S**
**Boston ◆ New York**

Manufactured in the United States of America.

6  5  4  3  2  1
f  e  d  c  b  a

*For information, write:* Bedford/St. Martin's, 75 Arlington Street, Boston, MA 02116   (617-399-4000)

ISBN: 978-1-4576-0217-7

# *Preface*

These additional exercises for *Successful College Writing* are meant to be a student's self-tutorial. Each exercise set includes clear instructions, and all sentence exercises include a hand-corrected example. The exercises are double-spaced to make revision easier. Answers and suggested responses are included in the answer key in the back of the booklet, making it easy for you to check your own work. Also included is a writing assessment, an appendix that will help you and your instructor determine aspects of your writing that you need to improve.

The exercises cover topics from Chapter 7, "Drafting an Essay" (Exercises P.1, P.2, and so on), Chapter 10, "Editing Sentences and Words" (Exercises E.1, E.2, and so on), and Part 7, "Handbook: Writing Problems and How to Correct Them" (the exercise numbers correspond to chapters in the handbook). They provide opportunities for you to practice crafting paragraphs, editing for sentence style and word choice, identifying parts of speech, and editing sentences for problems with grammar, punctuation, and mechanics. Also included is a section on ESL troublespots.

Interactive versions of these exercises and additional practices are also available online. Visit **http://bcs.bedfordstmartins.com/exercisecentral/Home.aspx** to access *Exercise Central* — Bedford/St. Martin's extensive electronic exercise bank.

# Contents

## ESL Troublespots  *70*

## Answers to Exercises  *79*

## Appendix: Writing Assessment  *107*

# PARAGRAPHS

**Name** _____ **Date** _____ **Section** _____

## Exercise P.1  Topic Sentences

Read the following sentences and determine which make effective topic sentences and which make poor or unfocused topic sentences. If the topic sentence is effective, write *effective*. If the topic sentence is poor or unfocused, rewrite the sentence so that it is an effective topic sentence for a paragraph.

For help with this exercise, see Chapter 6 in *Successful College Writing*.

**EXAMPLE:**

➤ Many Americans spend more than they earn.

*The widespread availability of credit cards allows many Americans to spend more than they earn and accumulate a lot of high-interest debt.*

1. Americans often wonder why obesity is not such a big problem in other countries.

   _____

   _____

2. Every Thursday, I take my dog Buster to the children's hospital to visit the patients.

   _____

   _____

3. The Boston Marathon is a very tough race that requires a lot of training.

   _____

   _____

4. People who choose high-stress jobs they do not enjoy in order to make a lot of money often find themselves unhappy and unsatisfied later in life.

   _____

   _____

5. Online dating is becoming more popular as a new way to meet people.

   _____

   _____

6. In the interest of closing the digital divide, several companies are currently developing inexpensive laptops to distribute to underprivileged school-children around the world.

   _____

   _____

7. Celebrities are given far too much attention in our culture.

   _____

   _____

8. Many Hollywood movies stereotype minorities and perpetuate limited, biased views of them.

   _____

   _____

9. I can no longer afford to visit national parks on my summer vacations because it's too expensive.

   _____

   _____

10. Because many drugs that children now take for depression and other mental illnesses have not been tested on children, we have no way of knowing whether their benefits outweigh their possible side effects.

    _____

    _____

## Exercise P.2  Topic Sentences

Each of the following paragraphs contains only supporting sentences. The paragraph may also contain a transitional sentence. Write an appropriate topic sentence in the space provided within each paragraph. (The thesis of the essay from which the paragraph is taken is provided for you.)

For help with this exercise, see Chapter 6 in *Successful College Writing.*

1. **Thesis:** A balanced-budget amendment to the U.S. Constitution is unnecessary and inappropriate.

    Proponents like to argue that a balanced-budget amendment would force the government to be more frugal, like ordinary citizens. _____

    _____

    If everyone who bought a house had to come up with the full price in cash, very few Americans would be homeowners. The same is true of cars, which are often financed through banks or automobile companies. Most people can't come up with $40,000 for a new sport-utility vehicle, so to get one, they borrow. In addition, keeping up with the Joneses is a time-honored tradition in this country. If our neighbors have a pool, we want a pool, too—and how do we pay for it? We use loans, credit cards, or other buy-now-pay-later financing.

2. **Thesis:** The lifestyle that many Americans enjoy contributes to poor health.

    Medical science has proved that people need exercise if they are to look and feel their best. _____

    _____

    Many people's parents and grandparents earned a living through physical labor. Today, most workers in this country don't have to exert themselves. In the past, people had to leave the house for entertainment. Now everyone has a television and a remote control, so no one has to get off the couch. When modern Americans do go out, they almost always drive to their destinations. Then, when they arrive, convenient parking and the increasing availability of elevators ensure that people walk no more than a few steps unless they choose to exert themselves.

3. **Thesis:** Parents should give their children the best possible start in life.

A child is capable of hearing sounds even before it is born. By the time a fetus is a few months old, it can respond to noises it hears. At birth, babies know the sound of their mothers' voices. But voices are not the only sounds infants can distinguish. Many parents also tell anecdotes about their children recognizing music that the parents played frequently before the children were born. While scientists do not yet know much about the way human brains learn before birth, they do know that when schoolchildren listen to music, especially classical music, their mathematical abilities often improve. Some neurologists speculate that exposure to music might affect the developing brain of a fetus as well. _____

_____

_____

Name _____ Date _____ Section _____

## Exercise P.3  Relevant Details

In each of the following paragraphs, underline any sentences containing details that do not support the topic sentence.

For help with this exercise, see Chapter 6 in *Successful College Writing*.

1.  (1) The long and interesting history of pinball spans a period from ancient times to the present. (2) The first game on record that can be considered an ancestor of modern pinball was an ancient Greek sport in which players rolled balls down a hill, trying to drop them in holes. (3) During the Renaissance, a tabletop version of the game, then called *bagatelle,* was invented. (4) A stick propelled the bagatelle balls up a tilted board filled with holes. (5) Interestingly, the word *bagatelle* can also refer to a short poem or piece of music. (6) In 1930, David Gottlieb designed a bagatelle board with a plunger, and modern pinball was born. (7) Later improvements included the "tilt" alarm, in 1933, and bumpers, in 1936. (8) Pinball was outlawed in some places during World War II because authorities likened it to gambling. (9) When the flipper was added to the game in 1947, pinball became more decidedly a game of skill, and eventually it became a legal, if not always reputable, sport across the country. (10) Pinball remains a common arcade game today, but more people probably play it as a computer game than in any other form.

2.  (1) Although big-budget disaster movies have depicted this scenario, the possibility that a meteor will strike the earth and cause significant damage and loss of human life is very remote. (2) Most meteors are relatively small, some (known as *micrometeors*) only the size of a grain of rice. (3) These meteors burn up as soon as they enter the earth's atmosphere. (4) According to folklore, when observers see one of these "shooting stars," they should make a wish. (5) Vaporized matter from burned-out meteors adds about ten tons to the mass of the earth every day. (6) About 150 meteors per year actually do survive the trip to earth and strike it. (7) Most of these do no damage even if they hit a spot where people live. (8) Since most of the earth is covered with water, however, meteors are much more likely to land in the ocean.

(9) Scientists estimate that a deadly meteor strike—one large enough to kill a hundred people and positioned to strike a populated area—would occur no more often than every 100,000 years, so the average person doesn't need to worry much about such an event.

3.    (1) Working on a custom cutting crew is a difficult way to make a living, and it's getting harder all the time. (2) First of all, custom cutters—traveling workers who supply the machinery and labor to harvest farmers' crops as they ripen—are able to work only seasonally. (3) Running a family farm has never been easy. (4) Grain crops in the South begin to ripen in the spring, and cutting crews follow the harvest north as the weather warms throughout the summer; when the harvest is finished in August, the work is over for the year. (5) Nor is custom cutting an easy task: The work is hot, dirty, and difficult, and the hours are long. (6) To make matters worse, the machines needed to harvest grain are very expensive, so start-up costs for a custom cutting crew are prohibitive. (7) The expense of new harvesting machines, called combines, and the need to get the harvest in as quickly as possible are major reasons farmers hire custom cutters rather than doing the work themselves. (8) In addition, the amount of work available, and the wages to be earned from it, depend on the success of the farmer's crop. (9) This success, in turn, is dependent on factors beyond human control, such as the weather. (10) Finally, as small farmers become an increasingly rare breed, there is less and less need for custom cutting.

Name _____ Date _____ Section _____

## Exercise P.4 Paragraph Unity

Read through the following paragraphs and decide whether the paragraph is unified or not unified. If the paragraph is unified, write *unified* on the line following the paragraph. If the paragraph is not unified, write *not unified* and then eliminate the sentences that are off-topic.

For help with this exercise, see Chapter 8 in *Successful College Writing*.

**EXAMPLE:**

Most people believe that you can never drink too much water, but studies are now showing that drinking too much water can be very dangerous to your health. In fact, being overhydrated is much more dangerous than being dehydrated. ~~I try to drink eight glasses of water a day.~~ Overhydrating reduces the sodium levels in your blood and can cause confusion, seizures, and even death. ~~On very hot days, many people are in danger of becoming dehydrated. Dehydration is one of the factors that can contribute to heat stroke.~~ Athletes are actually better off waiting until they are thirsty and drinking only what their bodies can absorb.

_____ *not unified* _____

1.    One alternative to drugs for treating depression is the controversial Eye Movement Desensitization and Reprocessing or EMDR.  This treatment is particularly useful for people who are depressed as a result of a traumatic event.  Prozac is also useful for treating depression.  For those who don't respond to Prozac, doctors often recommend Zoloft.  In an EMDR session, the therapist makes hand motions or flashes a light in front of the patient's face while he or she talks about an upsetting experience.  People who have experienced trauma often need a lot of support.  Many people have found this nontraditional therapy to be very helpful in processing their experiences, though no one knows for sure why EMDR works. _____

2.    The advertisements that now appear before the movie are not effective because they only make moviegoers irritable. Coke is one of the most frequently advertised products and one of the most recognized American brands. People often drink Coke or other soft drinks when they go to the

movies. Ads take away from the otherwise enjoyable experience of seeing a movie in the theater. These days, you have to sit through ten minutes of commercials before the previews start. Advertisers also use product place-ment as a way to increase their product's visibility. By the time the movie begins, you may already have been in your seat for half an hour. Because of this inconvenience, people may decide that it's worthwhile to wait for the DVD and skip the ads. Movie-theater owners would be wise to remember their paying audience and reconsider this partnership with advertisers.

———————————

3.    Contrary to what a person might expect, training to become a clown takes a lot of hard work and dedication. Many clowns-in-training spend significant amounts of time learning their art at one of the many clown schools around the world.  These schools teach gesture, expression, and movement in addi-tion to make-up technique and costume design. Some schools specialize in training certain types of clowns, like the "character" clown or the "white-face" clown, and require that students focus on one style of clowning. In addition to choosing a focus and going to school, clowns must be disciplined in order to remain playful, curious, and physically limber. Goofiness is not as easy as it looks. ———————————

4.    One of America's most well-known and important court cases is the Scopes "Monkey Trial." Students should learn their country's history at an early age. Knowing the past can help us predict the future.  In 1925, John Scopes, a high school biology teacher, was charged with violating state law by teaching the theory of evolution to his students. He believed he was teaching an important scientific theory, but others believed that evolution contradicted the story of creation told in the Bible.  The trial became famous because so many people had such strong feelings on both sides. It has also remained rel-evant because we haven't come to a definitive conclusion about which ideas students should or should not learn in school. There are many old conflicts

that remain unresolved. For instance, people have been arguing for decades over whether or not abortion should be legal. _____

5.    More animal shelters should adopt a "no kill" policy. Controlling the stray animal population by euthanizing is not the best solution. Killing unwanted pets solves the problem of overpopulation only temporarily, and it creates a bigger problem because it teaches people that animals are disposable. Many people don't consider snakes, iguanas, and other reptiles as pets. When I was seven, I adopted a snake from our local shelter, and he turned out to be a wonderful pet. We need to learn to be kinder and more responsible when it comes to animals. We need to have pets fixed and accept them even when they have special needs. We need to accept humans with special needs as well. Many of the animals in shelters are there because they were neglected or mis-treated. If we change our own behavior, fewer animals will end up abused and unwanted. _____

6.    Buying a house is not always a good investment. People who sell their houses after owning them for only a couple of years often lose money. Spending money on a computer is not always a good investment either. Computers lose their value very quickly. Unless the buyer uses the computer for work, money spent on a computer is money lost. People who don't buy enough insurance for their homes can lose money if there is a fire, flood, or other disaster. Houses also require a lot of maintenance. When people sell their houses, often they find it difficult to make back the money they spent fixing up the house. Sometimes people are better off investing their money in something that does not cost so much. _____

7.    Keeping up with all the new developments in communications technology has become nearly impossible. Just knowing what is available takes many hours of research. A new cell phone with better reception and more features may be convenient in the long run, but finding out about it can be time-consuming and inconvenient. It's important to draw a line somewhere to

avoid becoming overwhelmed by all the new technology. When drawing the line, it's often best to let necessity be your guide. _____

8.    Hilary Swank is a positive role model for young actresses. Jennifer Lopez is a good role model for future dancers and singers. Many girls look up to their mothers as well. Unlike many successful women in the movie industry, Swank is not afraid to challenge herself when choosing roles. In both *Boys Don't Cry* and *Million Dollar Baby,* Swank focuses not on looking pretty but on inhabiting her characters and their difficult lives. Her determination and willingness to take these risks may come in part from her background. She was not born into a rich or privileged family and, like some of the characters she plays, has had to work very hard to achieve her goals. Many famous people have rough starts. Jennifer Lopez did not come from a rich family. It's important for young girls to see a successful movie star who has dedication, integrity, and a real love of acting. _____

## Exercise P.5  Specific Details

Rewrite each of the following vague, general paragraphs to include concrete, specific details. You may add new information and new sentences.

For help with this exercise, see Chapter 8 in *Successful College Writing.*

1.     A family gathering is supposed to be a happy occasion, but it may not be. Getting together for a family event can produce negative emotions just as often as positive ones. Just because people are related to each other doesn't mean they understand or like each other especially well. People usually try to be on their best behavior, but the strain of trying to be nice can make them tense. At a big gathering, there are bound to be relatives present who don't get along. Finally, if one of them snaps and an argument ensues, everyone else has bad feelings about the conflict.

2.     A movie can't be good unless all of the pieces come together successfully. Sometimes I see a film and think that the concept is great, but the script is just awful. I've seen other films with good scripts but bad acting. Then there are times when the pace is all wrong, and I wonder what the director was thinking. The music, too, can make or break a film. With so many variables, it's a wonder that any good movies exist. They do, of course; I could name two or three recent ones that did almost everything right.

3.     Children should have a pet. Taking care of a pet is a good experience for any child. For one thing, having a pet teaches children to assume responsibility. Additionally, pet care can teach children about loving and protecting a creature weaker than themselves. Both of these lessons are valuable for a child. Finally, a pet returns affection and can actually make a child's life happier. Most adults who had a pet in childhood believe that it was a positive experience.

For help with this exercise, see Chapter 8 in *Successful College Writing*.

## Exercise P.6  Paragraph Development

Read the following paragraphs and decide whether they are well developed or underdeveloped.  On the line after each paragraph write *well developed* if the paragraph is well developed and *underdeveloped* if it is underdeveloped. If you determine that the paragraph is underdeveloped, write three questions or suggestions that might help the writer develop his or her ideas more fully.

**EXAMPLES:**

➤    The number of children suffering from asthma has reached epidemic proportions over the last three decades. According to the Centers for Disease Control, over 7 million American children have been diagnosed with this chronic respiratory disease. Several factors have been blamed for this growing problem, though no clear cause is known. Air pollutants, such as ozone and sulfur dioxide, may play a role in the development of asthma. Indoor pollutants, such as dust mites, molds, animal dander, and tobacco smoke, may play an even bigger role. Some experts believe that the increased incidence of asthma is the direct result of children spending more time indoors exposed to these allergens. Whatever the cause, it is clear that children's developing lungs are particularly at risk. The number of asthma-related deaths in America has decreased every year since 2000, but until we know how to stop the epidemic completely, the best we can do is try to minimize exposure to dangerous environments and treat the life-threatening symptoms aggressively.

_____*well developed*_____

1. _____*If the paragraph is well developed, leave these lines blank.*_____

2. _____

3. _____

➤    Many developing countries are finding it easier to join the developed world by way of technological leapfrogging. Leapfrogging helps developing countries improve their technologies. This entails skipping the intermediate steps of technological development and starting instead with the most current technologies. For instance, an area that has never had phone service might decide it's more efficient to build cell phone towers rather than old-fashioned phone lines. Other areas might decide to install a wi-fi Internet connection, rather than running telephone lines for dial-up service. There are problems with leapfrogging, too, of course. It isn't the right solution for every agricultural economy looking to get up to speed. Sometimes, the old tried-and-true technologies have advantages.

_____*underdeveloped*_____

1. _Which countries are finding success with leapfrogging?_

2. _Identify several reasons why a country might choose to leapfrog._

3. _Describe a situation in which leapfrogging would not be advisable and explain why not._

1.    Children's museums are growing faster than any other kind of museum in the country. Parents like museums where their children are allowed to touch and interact with the exhibits. Other museums rely on seeing objects and reading information, which can become tiresome for children. Children's museums are usually educational as well. They introduce kids to many different things, as well as allowing them a fun, safe place to play. Museums are a great place for children to learn about anatomy, geology, and astronomy. Some of the best children's museums are in big cities like Boston and Cleveland. It's interesting that children's museums are growing faster than natural history museums or aquariums, places that also specialize in children's exhibits.

    _____

1. _____

2. _____

3. _____

2.    Though the methods have improved somewhat over the last century, coal mining is still a very dangerous way to make a living. Coal miners are more likely to die on the job than workers in nearly any other occupation, the obvious exception being soldiers in the military. Even the well-organized coal miners' union cannot protect workers from some of the industry's unavoidable hazards. Some people wonder why anyone would do this kind of work. Many people work in coal mines because it's what their fathers and their fathers' fathers did. It's tradition. Some would even argue that the danger of the job is part of the coal miner's tradition. Tradition or not, the government should do more to protect workers from society's necessary but hazardous jobs.

    _____

1. _____

2. _____

3. _____

3.    Starting with her debut single "Tim McGraw" and the release of a self-titled album, Taylor Swift brought country music back onto the playlist of

American pop. Country music as a genre has rarely made it onto the mainstream music charts, which in recent years have favored the metallic sounds of rock and the lively rhythms of pop. Swift incorporates these elements into her songs, but remains a country musician at heart. Alongside electric bass lines and pop style beats, Swift recalls her Nashville roots with twanging banjos and soaring fiddle parts. This artful melding of genres and styles gives her music mainstream appeal as well as uniqueness. Critics praise Swift also for her barefaced honesty in her lyrics, which address topics such as love and heartbreak with refreshing frankness—all sung in Swift's signature country accent. Swift's beautiful musical blending has earned her multiple Grammy Awards, including the honor of being the only solo country act ever to win Best Album of the Year.

_____

1. _____

2. _____

3. _____

4.   Soap making is a fun and fascinating process. People have been making soap in one way or another for thousands of years. Because most people these days buy their soap at the store, very few of us know how soap is made. In fact, the process hasn't changed much over the years. The basic principles are the same. Most soaps are made by combining two or three things that are easy to get. By adding a few extra ingredients like eggs, you can even make a decent shampoo. It's strange to think that egg could be used to clean your hair. Unfortunately, soap making has gained a somewhat sinister reputation because of movies like *Fight Club*. This reputation is completely undeserved, as any investigation into the subject and the product would quickly reveal. Perhaps if more people took the time to learn how to make soap, they would realize how enjoyable and useful it can be.

_____

1. _____

2. _____

3. _____

5.   It is unlikely that any baseball team will ever match the comeback that the Boston Red Sox achieved in the 2004 American League Championship Series. Behind three games to zero, the Red Sox came back to win four straight games and beat the seemingly unbeatable New York Yankees. No team in the history of baseball had ever come back from being three games behind to

win a postseason series. The fact that the Red Sox achieved this while playing their archrivals only made the victory more memorable. What most baseball fans will remember most, though, is how the Red Sox rode the wave of their playoff comeback. They went on to win the World Series for the first time in eighty-six years. That's a comeback story that will be hard to beat.

_____

1. _____
2. _____
3. _____

6.     In the past couple of decades, political discourse has gotten so ugly that some Americans have taken to calling it the "inCivil War." YourDictionary.com even named "inCivility" the Word of the Year in 2004. The problem with incivility is that it usually sparks a chain reaction. The chain reaction leads to an escalation of the conflict, making mountains out of molehills. People have a difficult time responding politely to uncivil comments and thus spark more uncivil comments. As a result, public discourse has taken on a shrill, adversarial tone. This tone is not constructive and just results in more conflict. Unfortunately, we seem to pay more attention to those speakers who are confrontational and offensive.

_____

1. _____
2. _____
3. _____

7.     "The New Black" may be the most overused phrase in the fashion industry. Every color, at one point or another, has taken its turn being the new black. Even black has been the new black. The question that no one seems to be asking is, Why does black need to be replaced, anyway? Black is for more than just funerals. Urban working women, in particular, have found black to be very useful. They have discovered that wearing black is a good way to look formal and chic without a lot of effort. Also, owning a lot of black clothes reduces the amount of time a person has to spend worrying about whether or not her clothes match.

_____

1. _____
2. _____
3. _____

8.    Teenagers who ride their skateboards on city sidewalks create a hazard for everyone. Many passersby are injured every year by skateboarders who are riding in prohibited areas and/or riding too fast. I know several people who have collided or nearly collided with a skateboarder in a pedestrian zone. This can be very dangerous. Several of these incidents resulted in minor injuries to both the skateboarder and the pedestrian. Often, skateboarders are looking to practice their skills and are not simply trying to get from one point to another. They should find other places to practice so that the sidewalks are safe for the rest of us.

_____

1. _____

2. _____

3. _____

## Exercise P.7  Transitions and Repeated Words

Add transitions, repeat key words, or add synonyms as necessary to make the following paragraphs coherent and connected.

For help with this exercise, see Chapter 8 in *Successful College Writing*.

1.    The French may still have the international reputation of being the people most interested in gourmet food. Americans are quickly gaining an interest in gourmet food. "American food" meant fast foods like hamburgers and hot dogs. People around the world still associate these foods with American culture. U.S. food lovers may seek out the best burgers, fries, and barbecue foods. They also want to sample foods from ethnic cultures within the United States and other countries. People want the best of what American produce has to offer and will go far to find fresh, local ingredients that are expertly prepared.

2.    Modern conceptions of timekeeping owe a lot to the ancient Babylonians. The ancient Babylonians gave people today the twelve-month year, the twenty-four-hour day, the sixty-minute hour, and the sixty-second minute. The number *twelve* was significant to the ancient Babylonians. They noticed that there were usually twelve full moons in a year. The Babylonian calendar contained twelve months of thirty days each. Five days were left over each year; every six years they had to add an extra month to the year. They divided the day and night into twelve hours each. The number *sixty* was important to the Babylonians. The number *sixty* can be evenly divided by many integers — two, three, four, five, six, ten, twelve, fifteen, twenty, and thirty. They divided each hour into sixty minutes and each minute into sixty seconds. The Romans changed the length of some Babylonian months from thirty to thirty-one or twenty-eight days. The Babylonians' other time measurements survive to this day.

3.    The Restoration period in England, which began with the return of the monarchy in 1660, was marked by the kind of public behavior on the part of aristocrats and courtiers that would still provoke a shocked reaction today.

King Charles II served as the model of moral — or immoral — behavior for members of his court. There were no children by his wife. He had a large number of children by his several mistresses. Young male courtiers boasted of numerous love affairs. Court poets and dramatists composed bawdy, amoral literary works. Many contained words and suggestions that even modern newspapers would not print. The public loved to attend performances of plays. Simply being seen at a theater could give a person a questionable reputation. The clergy and other representatives of moral authority protested the literary, theatrical, and personal misbehavior of the aristocrats. Bawdiness became less fashionable. A much more conservative age followed the Restoration.

## Exercise P.8  Outlining

Read through the partially completed outline below. Then read through the list of missing notes/phrases that follow. Identify which note or phrase goes in which blank in order to best complete the outline. There are ten phrases and ten blanks, so you will need to use all ten phrases in order to complete the outline.

For help with this exercise, see Chapter 7 in *Successful College Writing.*

| Title | **More Than Just a Place to Sleep** |
|---|---|
| **Introduction** | *Thesis:* Though it requires some preparation and adaptability, staying at a traditional Japanese hotel, or *ryokan,* is an enjoyable and worthwhile way for a Western visitor to learn about Japanese culture. |

**Body Paragraph 1**   Finding a *ryokan*

- _____

- determine your price range

- _____

- make advance reservations

**Body Paragraph 2**   Apparel etiquette in a *ryokan*

- take off your shoes when you enter the *ryokan* and put on slippers

- _____

- wear *geta* (wooden clogs) if you stroll around the *ryokan* grounds

- _____

- _____

- wear a *tanzen* (outer robe) over your *yukata* if you get cold

**Body Paragraph 3**   Japanese bath etiquette

- the Japanese often bathe before dinner

- in changing room, put *yukata* in basket provided

- _____

- do not drain the water from the tub when finished

- _____

**Body Paragraph 4**    Engaging with your host or hosts

- learn a few key phrases in Japanese

- ask about the building and garden

- _____

**Body Paragraph 5**    A day in the life of a different culture

- _____

- enjoy the serenity of life without television

- try meditating

- _____

**Conclusion**    While staying in a familiar Western-style hotel might feel easier, after a night or two in a *ryokan* you'll find yourself more mindful of Japanese culture and traditions, and remarkably refreshed.

1. be willing to try unusual breakfast foods, like cold squid and miso soup

2. decide how formal or informal a *ryokan* you'd like

3. take off the slippers when walking on the tatami mats

4. wear your *yukata* (robe provided by the *ryokan*) when in the *ryokan*

5. ask about the best sights to see in their town

6. locate Web sites that list *ryokans*

7. *yukatas* should be worn left side over right; right side over left is for funerals

8. dry yourself thoroughly before returning to the changing room

9. wash yourself in the bathing area using shower or basin before entering the public bath

10. adjust to the firmness of a futon mattress

## EDITING SENTENCES AND WORDS

**Name** _____ **Date** _____ **Section** _____

### Exercise E.1  Wordy Sentences

Revise the following sentences to make them as concise as possible.

For help with this exercise, see Chapter 10 in *Successful College Writing*.

**EXAMPLE:**

➤ ~~At some point in time~~ ^E^ʸ́very year, a list of the most popular names ~~for children~~ ^children's^ in the United States is published.

1. It seems likely that American parents choose really carefully when naming their children.

2. Making comparisons between popular names of today and the names that were popular in the past shows how much our ideas about naming children have changed.

3. The names chosen for girls have undergone the most changes.

4. Forty years ago, the majority of baby girls received names that sounded traditional rather than being considered unusual.

5. Some of the older names gradually became less popular over a period of time, and newer names, like Jennifer, now a perennial favorite year after year, took their place.

6. In these modern times, parents often give their daughters names that were once considered masculine, like Sidney or Taylor.

7. It is also true that some parents try to make their daughters' names seem quite unusual by spelling a traditional name in a way that is not considered traditional.

8. Boys' names, however, have really changed very little and not as noticeably.

9. For decades the most popular of the names parents have given to boys has been Michael.

10. It may perhaps be true, as the results of a recent poll suggest, that parents think having an unusual name is helpful to girls and having an unusual name is harmful to boys.

For help with
this exercise, see
Chapter 10 in
*Successful College
Writing.*

## Exercise E.2  Combining Sentences

Combine each of the following pairs of sentences to create a compound or complex sentence.

**EXAMPLE:**

➤ Many people start smoking as teenagers, ~~They~~ *because they* think it makes them look mature.

1. Nicotine is an ingredient in cigarettes. It is an addictive drug.

2. No smoker sets out to become addicted to cigarettes. Most people have difficulty stopping once they start smoking.

3. Movies can affect young people profoundly. Movies often portray smokers as glamorous and sexy.

4. Many thirty-year-old people do not smoke. They are unlikely to begin smoking.

5. The tobacco companies need new customers. They are more apt to find such customers among the younger generations.

6. Some teenagers take up smoking. They don't consider the possible consequences.

7. The Joe Camel cartoon advertisements were controversial. Cartoons often appeal to children.

8. The Joe Camel advertising campaign was withdrawn. New restrictions have been placed on tobacco ads.

9. Smoking can be unsightly and unhealthy. It is legal.

10. The number of lawsuits against tobacco companies has risen recently. Families have argued that tobacco companies are to blame for the deaths of their loved ones.

## Exercise E.3  Adding Modifiers

Revise each sentence by adding the modifiers in any appropriate place.

For help with this exercise, see Chapter 10 in *Successful College Writing*.

**EXAMPLE:**

➤ Scientists have studied criminal behavior.

[*Modifiers:* hoping to find ways to prevent crime; for many years]

*Revised:* For many years, scientists have studied criminal behavior, hoping to find ways to prevent crime.

1. Criminal tendencies were thought to be related to physical traits. [*Modifiers:* in the nineteenth century; mistakenly]

2. Phrenologists mapped the human head. [*Modifiers:* who studied bumps on the skull; for antisocial protrusions]

3. They hoped. [*Modifiers:* before crimes occurred; that they could identify potential criminals]

4. Other researchers measured the proportions of the human head. [*Modifiers:* followers of a pseudoscience called craniometry; carefully recording their findings]

5. Craniometrists inferred conclusions. [*Modifiers:* using measurements of skull circumference; about brain size and intelligence as well as criminality]

6. These scientists' studies were fatally flawed. [*Modifiers:* from the beginning; because they found what they expected to find]

7. Researchers have been focusing on psychology. [*Modifiers:* since these "sciences" fell out of favor in the mid-twentieth century; as a means of understanding criminal actions]

8. The debate continues. [*Modifiers:* over which influence is stronger, heredity or environment; among social scientists]

9. The issue may never be resolved. [*Modifiers:* one of the key controversies among scientists; to everyone's satisfaction]

10. Important questions generate useful research. [*Modifiers:* In scientific inquiry; as well as theories that are later discredited; however]

## Exercise E.4  Parallelism

Correct any errors in parallelism in the following sentences.

For help with
this exercise, see
Chapter 10 in
*Successful College
Writing.*

**EXAMPLE:**

➤ Americans should investigate renewable energy sources, including solar heat and
*wind power.*
~~power from the wind.~~
‸

1. The United States uses large amounts of energy, is depending heavily on oil,
   and imports much of that oil.

2. Burning oil for energy pollutes the air, destroys an irreplaceable commodity,
   and is wasting resources.

3. During the 1970s, an embargo made oil expensive and it was not easy to get.

4. The oil crisis led to a wider interest in alternative energy sources that would
   be renewable, environmentally sound, and would cost less than oil.

5. Some new homes used solar heating, although it was expensive to install
   and despite its being still relatively untested.

6. Many Americans expected electric cars to be perfected and that they would
   be widely available by the end of the twentieth century.

7. Instead, the embargo ended, the cost of oil dropped, and there were declin-
   ing gasoline prices.

8. At the same time, money to invent alternative energy technologies, to
   develop new products, and for marketing the products dried up.

9. Scientists and those who study the environment hope that there will be
   plentiful renewable energy sources someday.

10. It would be better to have alternative energy possibilities soon than waiting
    for the world's oil reserves to run dry.

For help with
this exercise, see
Chapter 10 in
*Successful College
Writing.*

## Exercise E.5  Strong, Active Verbs

Revise the following sentences by using strong, active verbs.

**EXAMPLE:**

➤ ~~There are major fashion shows~~ every year in cities like Paris, Milan, and New York.
   *Fashion designers parade their wares*

1. Big crowds are drawn to annual "Fashion Week" events in American and European cities.

2. Shows by new and established designers are attended by photographers, journalists, models, and celebrities.

3. Many people in the audience have model-thin bodies and photogenic faces.

4. Often, *haute couture* shows with their expensive, trend-setting fashions are the highlight of the event.

5. *Haute couture* garments are not expected to be worn by ordinary people.

6. *Haute couture* creations are frequently more like works of art than mere outfits.

7. Such clothing can be worn in public only by runway models.

8. Other people seem ridiculous in *haute couture* clothes.

9. Clothes can be draped more easily on models who have very thin bodies.

10. Some people are more impressed by the spectacle than by the clothes.

## Exercise E.6  Word Choice

Edit the following paragraph for appropriate diction and connotation.

*For help with this exercise, see Chapter 10 in* Successful College Writing.

**EXAMPLE:**

>                   *wealthy*
> ➤ From middle-class to ~~rich~~ American communities, the disease known as anorexia
> is on the rise.

    Americans have recently had their noses rubbed in the fact that anorexia nervosa, a disease of self-starvation, is becoming more widespread. Anorexia sufferers are overwhelmingly made up of teenage girls and young women. Most of them are white and come from middle-class or upper-class families. They are also usually sharp. They seem to other people to have pretty much every advantage. Their families and comrades ordinarily have a rough time comprehending why they will not eat. Because anorexia is a psychological disorder, the sufferers themselves may not catch on to what caused the onset of their illness. Anorexics have a weird body image. They often believe they are totally overweight unless they are dangerously slender. The disease is notoriously difficult to treat, even if the patient tries to go along with her doctors.

For help with this exercise, see Chapter 10 in *Successful College Writing.*

## Exercise E.7  Concrete, Specific Detail

Revise the following sentences by adding concrete, specific details.

**EXAMPLE:**

➤ Learning about ~~standardized tests~~ may improve a student's performance on them.
  *the types of questions featured on standardized tests such as the SAT and ACT*

1. Every year, a large number of high school students take standardized tests.

2. A good test score can help a student.

3. Test-preparation courses are becoming popular.

4. These courses are expensive.

5. Experts disagree about the value of such courses.

6. Many students get better scores after taking a course.

7. The amount of improvement is not always significant.

8. Opponents argue that the courses are unfair.

9. Others say that the courses make no real difference.

10. Many people continue to pay for test preparation.

## Exercise E.8 Figures of Speech

Edit the following sentences to eliminate clichéd words and expressions.

For help with this exercise, see Chapter 10 in *Successful College Writing*.

**EXAMPLE:**

➤ A woman athlete may have to work like a ~~mule~~ *marathon runner heading uphill* to earn her share of recognition.

1. For generations, women were considered to be delicate flowers too fragile for sports.

2. Many people thought that women would die like an old tree if they were too physically active.

3. Even though these mistaken beliefs were widespread, women athletes have moved forward by leaps and bounds.

4. Individual women athletes, like the track and golf star Babe Didrikson Zaharias, had to be as strong as an ox.

5. During World War II, a women's baseball league drew spectators like a snake in the grass when a shortage of male players depleted men's teams.

6. The end of the war nipped the women's league in the bud.

7. The American women's movement of the 1970s was the dawn of a new era for women in sports.

8. A "battle of the sexes" took place in tennis during that decade, when Billie Jean King, a star female player, made Bobby Riggs, an avowed "male chauvinist" who had challenged her, look as weak as the ocean tides.

9. In the following decades, some individual women became sports heroes, like Florence Griffith Joyner, who could run like the wind.

10. Finally, in the 1990s, the popularity of women's basketball and soccer spread like a disease in a crowded city.

For help with this exercise, see Chapter 10 in *Successful College Writing*.

## Exercise E.9  Weak Verb/Noun Combinations

Edit the following sentences to eliminate weak verb/noun combinations.

**EXAMPLE:**

➤ For many years, mentally ill people were ~~given the same treatment~~ *treated the same* as criminals.

1. The treatment of mental illness has been troublesome to societies throughout history.

2. A thousand years ago, observers thought mental disturbance offered proof that the sufferer was possessed by demons.

3. Many mentally ill people suffered death in the course of treatment for demonic possession.

4. Belief in demonic possession eventually underwent a decrease in much of the world.

5. Instead, doctors and others made a classification of mental illness as a kind of disease.

6. Sufferers were frequently put into confinement and, often, forgotten.

7. Officials made the decision that mentally ill people were antisocial, not sick.

8. Most healthy people rarely gave any consideration to the mentally ill.

9. In the nineteenth century, a reformer, Dorothea Dix, made an investigation into the treatment of the mentally ill in Massachusetts.

10. Her report shocked people so much that Massachusetts, and soon other states, passed legislation requiring humane treatment for sufferers of mental illness.

# PARTS OF SPEECH

**Name** _____ **Date** _____ **Section** _____

## Exercise 1.1  Nouns, Pronouns, and Verbs

Identify the underlined word as a noun, a pronoun, or a verb.

For help with this exercise, see handbook sections 1a-1c in *Successful College Writing*.

**EXAMPLE:**

➤ Many Americans don't realize how much <u>their</u> ignorance of number concepts *pronoun* affects their lives.

1. The mathematician John Allen Paulos <u>claims</u> that too many Americans do not understand basic mathematical ideas.

2. Paulos calls this <u>lack</u> of understanding "innumeracy."

3. Innumerates may not <u>grasp</u> the idea of probability.

4. <u>Failing</u> to understand the likelihood of an event may cause poor judgment.

5. Unreasonable fears—for example, of being killed in a terrorist attack—may paralyze citizens <u>who</u> don't appreciate how unlikely such an event is.

6. A related misunderstanding is the failure to realize how common coincidences <u>are</u>.

7. For instance, the chance of two strangers on an airplane having <u>acquaintances</u> in common is surprisingly high.

8. In addition, probability shows that in any random group of twenty-three people, there is a 50 percent chance that two of <u>them</u> share a birthday.

9. People unfamiliar with rules of probability <u>may</u> be dangerously gullible.

10. Educational reforms and a systematic <u>attempt</u> to show the fun side of math could help Americans overcome their number resistance.

For help with this exercise, see handbook section 1c in *Successful College Writing*.

## Exercise 1.2  Verb Form

Correct any errors in verb form in the following sentences. Some sentences may be correct as written.

**EXAMPLE:**

➤ In recent years, the study of detective stories ~~have~~ *has* become a legitimate academic pursuit.

1. Parents in the early twentieth century was warned that detective magazines could warp children's minds.

2. Pulp fiction about crime did indeed became rather lurid.

3. The detective story does, however, boast a literary past.

4. Many scholars have gave Edgar Allan Poe credit for being the first author to write detective fiction in English.

5. Poe's story "The Murders in the Rue Morgue" features an almost supernaturally clever detective.

6. Poe's detective clearly laid the foundation for the most famous literary sleuth, Sherlock Holmes.

7. In dozens of stories, Holmes, assisted by his friend Dr. Watson, uncovers the truth by careful observation.

8. Arthur Conan Doyle, the creator of Holmes and Watson, were amazed at the popularity of his fictional characters.

9. Some of the best-known writers of detective fiction in the twentieth century have been women.

10. While not all detective stories are worthy of serious study, the best ones are consider by scholars to be very rewarding.

## Exercise 1.3 Verb Tense

Identify the tense of each underlined verb.

For help with this exercise, see handbook section 1c in *Successful College Writing.*

**EXAMPLE:**

*past perfect progressive*

➤ By the spring of 1999, Wayne Gretzky <u>had been playing</u> professional hockey for over twenty years.

1. Wayne Gretzky <u>began playing</u> hockey in his native Canada at the age of three.

2. When he was five, he was frequently <u>scoring</u> goals against players several years older than he was.

3. Hockey fans <u>have known</u> Gretzky's name since his record-setting seasons with the Edmonton Oilers.

4. Before the Oilers traded him to Los Angeles, Gretzky <u>had acquired</u> his nickname, the "Great One."

5. Gretzky <u>holds</u> or shares more than sixty hockey records, an unprecedented number.

6. Several of his scoring records <u>will</u> probably always <u>stand</u>.

7. Gretzky's decision to retire in 1999 disappointed his fans, although they <u>had</u> perhaps <u>expected</u> the news.

8. When he retired, most of his fans <u>had been watching</u> him play for most of their lives.

9. Gretzky has said that he <u>will be spending</u> more time with his family now that his playing days are over.

10. In recognition of his achievements, the National Hockey League will never again <u>assign</u> a player Gretzky's number, 99.

For help with
this exercise, see
handbook section
1c in *Successful
College Writing.*

## Exercise 1.4  Verb Mood

Identify the mood — indicative, imperative, or subjunctive — of the underlined verb or verb phrase in each of the following sentences.

**EXAMPLE:**

➤ Charles Darwin's *The Origin of Species* <u>has inspired</u> *indicative* considerable discussion since its publication in 1859.

1. The study of biology <u>would be</u> very different today if Darwin had never written.

2. Although the mechanics of evolution <u>are</u> still <u>debated</u>, biologists all over the world accept Darwin's ideas.

3. Readers of Darwin's work in the nineteenth and early twentieth centuries <u>were</u> not easily <u>convinced</u>.

4. Many people wish that Darwin's theory <u>were</u> not widely accepted among scientists.

5. In the United States in 1925, a court of law told a Darwinian, "<u>Stop teaching</u> evolution."

6. In that famous trial, the Tennessee teacher J. T. Scopes <u>was tried</u> for telling his students to read about Darwin's theory.

7. Darrow argued that students <u>be</u> told.

8. The court ruled that the truth of evolutionary theory was not relevant, since Tennessee law <u>forbade</u> teaching it.

9. Scopes, who admitted teaching evolutionary theory, <u>lost</u> the case.

10. The Tennessee law forbidding the teaching of evolution <u>was</u> not <u>overturned</u> until 1967.

## Exercise 1.5 Adjectives and Adverbs

Identify the underlined word as an adjective or an adverb.

For help with this exercise, see handbook section 1d and 1e in *Successful College Writing.*

**EXAMPLE:**

➤ Education experts in the United States are debating the pros and cons of
   *adjective*
   <u>standardized</u> testing.

1. How <u>well</u> do American students compare with those in other industrialized nations?

2. A student who receives the <u>best</u> education the United States offers is likely to be very well prepared.

3. However, many students, especially those in <u>poorer</u> neighborhoods, get substandard training.

4. Education professionals agree that the U.S. <u>educational</u> system has problems.

5. <u>Unfortunately</u>, they cannot agree on what to do to solve this problem.

6. One <u>proposed</u> solution involves nationwide standards.

7. With nationwide standards, students across the country would be <u>responsible</u> for learning the same curriculum as all other students in the United States.

8. Students could prove they had met the standards by performing <u>satisfactorily</u> on a standardized test.

9. Supporters of <u>this</u> method claim that standards would force students to master knowledge before being promoted or graduating.

10. Some opponents argue that students learn <u>more</u> easily when teachers are able to use their own judgment about the curriculum.

For help with
this exercise, see
handbook sections
1f and 1g in
*Successful College
Writing.*

## Exercise 1.6  Conjunctions and Prepositions

Identify the underlined word or words as a form of a conjunction or a preposition.

**EXAMPLE:**

➤ A new rapidly growing branch <u>of</u> physics is chaos theory.
　　　　　　　　　　　　　　*preposition*

1. <u>For</u> about the last twenty years, physicists have been analyzing chaos.

2. <u>In spite of</u> common perceptions, chaos may not be completely random.

3. The operations of some incompletely understood biological systems — brains, <u>for example</u> — may thrive in the gray area between order and chaos.

4. Some physicists believe that apparently chaotic behavior may actually act <u>according to</u> patterns.

5. <u>If</u> chaos is somehow systematic, it is nevertheless tremendously complex.

6. Finding the patterns of chaotic behavior is sometimes possible, <u>although</u> identifying them is difficult.

7. One difficulty lies <u>in</u> determining the type of model appropriate for a given complex system.

8. Understanding these complex systems <u>not only</u> is interesting in theory, <u>but also</u> has potential practical uses.

9. One group of physicists has tried to understand the abstractions of chaos theory <u>and</u> make concrete gains from their knowledge.

10. <u>As</u> part of an attempt to predict its future behavior, they are studying the complex and chaotic system known as the stock market.

# SENTENCE STRUCTURE

Name _____ Date _____ Section _____

For help with this exercise, see handbook section 2a in *Successful College Writing*.

## Exercise 2.1  Subjects and Predicates

Identify the underlined portion of each sentence as a simple subject, a simple predicate, a complete subject, or a complete predicate.

**EXAMPLE:**
*simple subject*
➤ <u>What</u> makes one violin sound different from another?

1. <u>The making of violins</u> is an art that has been practiced for centuries.

2. Modern technological <u>advances</u> have hardly touched violin makers, known as luthiers.

3. The greatest violin makers of all time <u>worked two to three hundred years ago in Italy</u>.

4. Modern luthiers <u>still do not know exactly how those great violin makers—notably Stradivarius and Amati—produced such perfect instruments</u>.

5. <u>Stradivarius violins, only about 150 of which are known to exist today</u>, can be worth over a million dollars each.

6. Stradivarius, who worked in Cremona, Italy, <u>invented</u> the proportions of the modern violin.

7. Some experts <u>believe</u> that the shape of his violins produces their exquisite tone.

8. Others argue that the precise shape could be reproduced by modern methods, yet nobody <u>has succeeded so far in duplicating the famous Stradivarius sound</u>.

9. Another <u>theory</u> is that the maple wood Stradivarius used, which came from ancient trees in short supply today, gives his violins their tone.

10. Chemists <u>are experimenting</u> with ways to treat newer wood that might give violins the elusive resonance of a Stradivarius.

For help with
this exercise, see
handbook section
2a in *Successful
College Writing*.

## Exercise 2.2 Objects and Complements

Identify each underlined word as a direct object, an indirect object, a subject complement, or an object complement.

**EXAMPLE:**

*indirect object*

➤ Can computers give adult <u>brains</u> new capacities for learning foreign languages?

1. Some kinds of learning get <u>easier</u> as people grow older.

2. But most adults find learning a foreign language extremely <u>difficult</u>.

3. At birth, babies' brains can distinguish every <u>sound</u> in every human language.

4. As they grow, children's brains become less <u>able</u> to recognize different sounds.

5. After the age of ten, most people cannot acquire a foreign <u>language</u> without an accent.

6. Adult brains reinforce familiar <u>sounds</u> when they hear unfamiliar ones.

7. This phenomenon actually makes adults less <u>likely</u> to distinguish unfamiliar sounds with increased exposure.

8. An experimental computer simulation may give <u>adults</u> new abilities to learn unfamiliar language sounds.

9. The computer offers <u>students</u> a chance to hear the unfamiliar sounds in an exaggerated way.

10. Perhaps someday adult learners will also be fluent, unaccented <u>speakers</u> of foreign languages.

## Exercise 2.3  Phrases

Identify the underlined phrase in each sentence as a prepositional phrase, a verbal phrase, an appositive phrase, or an absolute phrase.

For help with this exercise, see handbook section 2b in *Successful College Writing*.

**EXAMPLE:**

                 *verbal phrase*

➤   The science <u>of analyzing human DNA</u> has become very precise in recent years.

1.  DNA, <u>the genetic code,</u> is a unique marker that is different in every human being.

2.  DNA analysis can be used <u>as a crime-fighting tool.</u>

3.  Like fingerprints, DNA <u>left at a crime scene</u> can help to identify a wrongdoer.

4.  Today, most people contemplating a crime know how <u>to avoid leaving fingerprints.</u>

5.  But criminals, <u>their DNA contained in every cell of their bodies,</u> can hardly avoid leaving identifying markers behind.

6.  Any clue — <u>a single hair, a trace of saliva</u> — can eventually convict a criminal.

7.  <u>A suspect having left a used coffee cup during questioning,</u> a police officer may not even need another sample to link him or her to the crime.

8.  The good news <u>for some people</u> charged with or convicted of a crime is that DNA can also prove someone not guilty.

9.  Some convicted criminals, <u>steadfastly maintaining their innocence,</u> have undergone new, sophisticated DNA analysis after years of imprisonment.

10. Recently, two men, <u>prisoners on death row,</u> were released after DNA tests proved they could not have committed the murder for which they were convicted.

For help with
this exercise, see
handbook section
2c in *Successful
College Writing*.

## Exercise 2.4  Subordinate Clauses

Underline the subordinate clause or clauses in each of the following sentences.

**EXAMPLE:**

➤  Superstitions, <u>which are irrational beliefs in charms and omens</u>, still have a hold
on modern life.

1.  Many superstitions date from classical or medieval times, when belief in
witchcraft was widespread.

2.  Superstitions were a way for people to explain whatever threatened them.

3.  Because cats were believed to be witches in disguise, the fear of a black cat
crossing one's path came about.

4.  Walking under ladders has also long been considered unlucky; this superstition may survive because it protects pedestrians from falling objects.

5.  Some people attribute to the Christian story of the Last Supper, where  thirteen people were present, the origins of the superstitious fear of the number
thirteen.

6.  Wherever it began, fear of the number thirteen, or triskaidekaphobia, is still
prevalent enough for many tall modern buildings not to have a thirteenth
floor.

7.  Early Romans believed that sneezing was a sign of the plague, so they  feared
it.

8.  The method they invented to protect a sneezer was to say, "God bless you."

9.  In the United States today, it is common to say "God bless you" — or
"Gesundheit," which is German for "health" — following a sneeze.

10.  Superstitions from the past may seem silly today, but who knows what
strange customs of the present will be ridiculed in the future?

## Exercise 2.5  Sentence Types

Indicate whether each of the following sentences is a simple, a compound, a complex, or a compound-complex sentence.

For help with this exercise, see handbook section 2d in *Successful College Writing.*

**EXAMPLE:**

➤ While extremely muscular or very thin people are often portrayed as the American ideal, Americans are, on the average, heavier than ever.  *complex*

1. Models and beauty contest winners in the United States have become much thinner in the last fifty years.

2. The weight that most people consider ideal for their height has also adjusted downward since the middle of the twentieth century.

3. The media have recently become more aware of the unhealthy effect that overly thin models can have on people and are making an effort to depict more moderately sized models.

4. More and better nutritional information is available today, and most Americans know the right way to eat.

5. Yet the number of people who actually eat right and have positive body image seems to have declined.

6. Since people know it is not healthy to over- or undereat, why are both obesity and anorexia still national problems?

7. Part of the reason for obesity may be this nation's overall good fortune and abundance.

8. Most people rarely go without their favorite foods, and American favorites tend to be high in fat and calories.

9. On the other hand, the media's old image of "perfect" bodies might still be to blame for eating disorders and unhealthy dieting.

10. Despite the media's efforts to foster a culture of positive body image and controlled eating in America, many people in this country have yet to embrace a healthy medium when it comes to weight, and they struggle with every meal.

Name _____ Date _____ Section _____

For help with
this exercise, see
handbook section
3 in *Successful
College Writing*.

## Exercise 3.1  Sentence Fragments

Correct any sentence fragments in the following sentences. Some sentences may be correct as written.

**EXAMPLE:**

➤ Among the many treasures at Yale's library. The Voynich manuscript stands out.

1. There are older and more valuable manuscripts. Than the Voynich.

2. However, there is none more mysterious. The Voynich still puzzling scholars many years after its discovery.

3. This manuscript was written in a code. So far unable to solve it.

4. Because the origins of the manuscript are unclear; the puzzle is doubly difficult.

5. No one knows. What country it came from.

6. Therefore, it very hard to determine the language the code represents. This makes decoding it even more troublesome.

7. Handwriting specialists can only guess at its age. It may date back to the Middle Ages.

8. The writing does not resemble. Any letters that can be traced to a known alphabet.

9. The manuscript which contains many beautiful illustrations. Of plants, people, and other seemingly unrelated images.

10. Because the Voynich manuscript is such an intriguing mystery. That some scholars might actually be disappointed to learn all of its secrets.

## Exercise 4.1  Run-On Sentences and Comma Splices

Correct any run-on sentences and comma splices in the following sentences.

For help with this exercise, see handbook section 4 in *Successful College Writing*.

**EXAMPLE:**

➤ Before her death in 1980, Mae West had become an institution; she had been in show business for seven decades.

1. Mae West began as a child star the career of "Baby Mae" took off when she performed at a local Brooklyn theater's amateur night.

2. At the age of nineteen, West began performing on Broadway she shocked audiences in 1911.

3. The voluptuous West became known for her suggestive clothing, even more famous were her suggestive wisecracks.

4. Attending black jazz clubs had introduced her to a new dance movement she performed this "shimmy" on Broadway, and it became a trademark for her.

5. West was not satisfied for long with the theatrical roles she was offered writing her own plays was one way to find good parts.

6. In 1925, she wrote a play called *Sex*, no producer she contacted would bring it to the stage.

7. The following year, West produced the play herself, advertisements for *Sex* were banned.

8. Nevertheless, the show played for nine months until it was closed down by the Society for the Suppression of Vice, West was arrested and spent eight days in jail.

9. In the 1930s and 1940s, Mae West took her naughty humor to Hollywood, while there she made a series of hit films and often wrote her own screenplays.

10. West made her final films in the 1970s by that time Americans found her less scandalous, but her name was still a household word.

For help with this exercise, see handbook section 5 in *Successful College Writing*.

## Exercise 5.1 Subject-Verb Agreement

Correct any errors in subject-verb agreement in the following sentences. Some sentences may be correct as written.

**EXAMPLE:**

➤ African American heritage and the end of slavery ~~is~~ <sup>are</sup> celebrated every year on June 19.

1. The festival called "Juneteenth," which people once recognized only in a few southern areas of the United States, are now much more widespread.

2. The events Juneteenth commemorates occurred after the end of the Civil War.

3. The surrender of the Confederate States were made official at Appomattox Courthouse on April 9, 1865.

4. From that day on, the Confederacy and the Union was again a single country.

5. Neither the northern states nor the southern states was now legally able to permit slave-owning, which had been officially outlawed in the United States several years earlier.

6. However, not all of the former slaves were aware they had been legally freed.

7. The story from those long-ago days go that in Texas, slave owners murdered the messengers bringing word of emancipation.

8. Not until June 19, 1865, were the news able to reach the last group of Texas slaves.

9. Therefore, festivities marking the end of slavery are held not on April 9 each year, the anniversary of the South's surrender, but on June 19.

10. Today, people celebrating Juneteenth attends concerts, films, and other cultural events.

## Exercise 6.1  Verb Forms

Correct any errors in verb form in the following sentences.

For help with this exercise, see andbook section in *Successful llege Writing*.

**EXAMPLE:**

➤ In 1915, a group of artists ~~had~~ decided to turn their backs on the traditional art world.

1.  The horrors of World War I were convincing some artists that European society had to change radically.

2.  Their reaction at first consist of musical and performance events they called the Cabaret Voltaire.

3.  Soon, however, the most influential members of the group begun to focus on visual art.

4.  The name *Dada* was chosen at random by the artists.

5.  They rejected older artistic traditions, including avant-garde ideas that recently became popular.

6.  Instead, the Dadaists challenging the whole concept of art.

7.  Before the Dada movement had ended in 1923, several of the artists had experimented with random arrangements of materials.

8.  Sometimes they chose the material they use from items discarded by other people.

9.  One artist, Marcel Duchamp, even sat up ordinary objects at art shows, claiming that the act of choosing the objects made them art.

10. Dada was a rebellion, not an attempt to build a new tradition, so no identifiable stylistic legacy of the movement remain today.

For help with
this exercise, see
handbook sections
7a–7d in *Successful
College Writing.*

## Exercise 7.1  Pronoun Reference

Correct any instances of vague or unclear pronoun reference in the following sentences.

**EXAMPLE:**

*and this attitude*

➤ Many Americans express tremendous cynicism about the U.S. government, ~~which~~ is not good for the country.

1. In much political analysis, they say that public distrust of the U.S. government began with Watergate.

2. That scandal's continuing legacy may make it one of the most influential American events of the twentieth century.

3. Since the early 1970s, political scandals have rarely interested Americans; they often seem to have very little effect.

4. Journalists provided the American people with a lot of information about the Iran-Contra hearings, but they could not have cared less.

5. Most people were indifferent; could it have been the result of post–Watergate trauma?

6. If Americans expect politicians to be corrupt, it will not surprise or even interest them.

7. Ironically, the media's coverage of scandals seems to have made the public suspicious of them as well.

8. Cynicism about political and journalistic motives leads to apathy, and it can spread contagiously.

9. Many people are so apathetic that it makes them refuse to vote.

10. If people do not believe that they can make a difference in the political process, it makes the country less democratic.

## Exercise 7.2 Pronoun-Antecedent Agreement

Correct any errors in pronoun-antecedent agreement in the following sentences. Some sentences may be correct as written.

For help with this exercise, see handbook sections 7c–7g in *Successful College Writing*.

**EXAMPLE:**

➤ Human ~~lives~~ *life* is important, and more lives could be protected if more were known about deadly storms.

1. Meteorology has made many advances in the past few decades, but they still cannot answer a number of questions about tornadoes.

2. Every tornado has their own unique characteristics.

3. The science of tornado watching has its own system, the Fujita scale, for measuring storms from weakest (F0) to strongest (F5).

4. An F4 tornado or an F5 tornado can destroy everything in their path.

5. Scientists cannot predict precisely how strong any tornado will be before they happen.

6. One reason why meteorologists find it difficult to predict tornados is its many possible causes.

7. Tornados can form due to wind flow patterns, or it might be caused by other factors such as temperature, moisture, instability, and lift.

8. Improved meteorological technology and the skill to interpret data have made their contributions to tornado prediction.

9. Either a few extra minutes of warning or more information about a storm's power would prove their effectiveness in saving lives.

10. People who live in a tornado zone should always know where his or her nearest safe area is.

help with
s exercise, see
ndbook sections
–7m in *Successful
llege Writing.*

### Exercise 7.3  Pronoun Case

Correct any errors in pronoun case in the following sentences. Some sentences may be correct as written.

**EXAMPLE:**

➤ Much of American mythology concerns heroes ~~whom~~ *who* solved problems by using
violence.

1.  Us residents of the United States are considered by much of the rest of the world to be an unusually violent people.

2.  Many researchers have debated they're theories about violent behavior in this country.

3.  Did the popular myth of the "Wild West" influence we and our ancestors?

4.  Other industrialized nations and us have very different policies concerning guns.

5.  Guns played an important part in Western settlement, but other machines may have been more significant than they.

6.  Violence and justice are so intertwined for many Americans that disagreements between other people and they can erupt into fights.

7.  American entertainment is frequently violent, too, and some people worry that such violence affects us and our children.

8.  There are defenders of violent films, TV shows, and video games whom claim that entertainment reflects our tastes rather than influencing them.

9.  What makes us Americans so prone to violence?

10.  Sometimes it seems that our worst enemies are us.

## Exercise 8.1  Shifts

Correct any inappropriate shifts in the following sentences.

For help with this exercise, see handbook sections 8a–8g in *Successful College Writing*.

**EXAMPLE:**

➤ Some scholars have asked ~~did~~ <sup>whether</sup> African folk traditions influence<sub>d</sub> African American folklore.

1. West African villages have strong oral traditions in which the younger people are told stories by their parents and grandparents.

2. Way back before the Revolutionary War, slave traders forced ancestors of the people from those villages to come to the United States.

3. In their difficult new situation in this country, the Africans adapted their stories so that you could learn from them.

4. Although different stories had different messages, one kind of character comes up over and over again.

5. The character is cunning and clever; call him a "trickster."

6. The stories about Br'er Rabbit are good examples of folktales whose hero was a trickster.

7. Many of the other animals want to gobble up Br'er Rabbit, who has only his wits to protect him.

8. Yet in every story, Br'er Rabbit not only escapes but his enemies are made to appear foolish by him as well.

9. Trickster characters like Br'er Rabbit showed slaves who heard these stories that they, too, could triumph by using cleverness when foes surround them.

10. Today, folklorists are exploring how did early African Americans encourage each other by telling stories of tricksters outsmarting powerful enemies.

For help with
this exercise, see
handbook sections
8h–8j in *Successful
College Writing*.

## Exercise 8.2  Mixed Constructions

Correct any mixed constructions in the following sent⟨ ⟩.

**EXAMPLE:**

➤ A common misconception is the ~~ability~~ *idea that it is easy* to identify wh⟨ ⟩meone is telling a lie.

1. Most people think perceiving falsehoods are easy ⟨ ⟩ot.

2. They think that interpreting nonverbal signals sh⟨ ⟩ when someone is lying.

3. The fact that these signals, such as avoiding eye c⟨ ⟩ct or hesitating before
   answering a question, are habits of truthful peop⟨ ⟩well.

4. The reason liars are hard to identify is because n⟨ ⟩gle trait always proves
   that a person is lying.

5. Truthful people who are afraid they will not be b⟨ ⟩ed may act suspiciously
   is one problem with lie detection.

6. There are a few people are unusually good at ide⟨ ⟩ing liars.

7. However, perhaps because these people are attu⟨ ⟩ deceitful behavior may
   explain why they are not especially good at iden⟨ ⟩g truth-tellers.

8. Listening to a stranger's lies may be easier to de⟨ ⟩han a loved one's.

9. The better someone knows and likes another p⟨ ⟩ seems to make spotting
   lies more difficult.

10. Someone who finds it hard to believe that her ⟨ ⟩ds would try to deceive
    her is an understandable human characteristic⟨ ⟩

## Exercise 9.1  Adjectives and Adverbs

Correct any errors in the use of adjectives or adverbs in the following sentences.

For help with this exercise, see handbook section 9 in *Successful College Writing*.

**EXAMPLE:**

➤ People think of beauty different in different cultures.
<sub>ly</sub> (insertion mark between "different" and "in")

1. Many people go to a lot of trouble to look attractively.

2. In the United States, no one thinks a woman wearing high heels is dressed strange.

3. Many Americans even go to real extreme lengths, such as having surgery, to be beautiful.

4. People can see the strangeness of beauty rituals clearer if the rituals are unfamiliar.

5. For example, in China in past centuries, beautiful women had to have the tiniest feet.

6. To achieve this goal, families bound their daughters' feet so tight that the feet could not grow.

7. Subcultures within the United States also have their own standards of beauty that may seem odder to people who are not part of the subculture.

8. For many young Americans, tattoos and body piercing were the trendier fashion statements of the 1990s.

9. They might have argued that such beautification was no unusualer than plucking out one's eyebrows.

10. Parents, however, often felt vastly relief if their children reached adulthood without tattoos.

For help with
this exercise, see
handbook section
10 in *Successful
College Writing.*

## Exercise 10.1  Misplaced and Dangling Modifiers

Correct any misplaced or dangling modifiers in the following sentences.

**EXAMPLE:**

➤ The sports world has changed to reflect the *rapidly growing* number of young athletes. ~~rapidly growing~~.

1. Recently, several sports have gained popularity that no one had heard of thirty years ago.

2. With a name that suggests their dangerous allure, members of Generation X are attracted to these athletic events.

3. These "Generation X" games often involve going to inaccessible places, which include snowboarding and sky-surfing.

4. Snow activities are especially popular that can be done on remote mountaintops.

5. Some of these sports have become so widely accepted that participants can now compete in the Olympics, such as freestyle skiing and snowboarding.

6. Gasping at the antics of snowboarders, mountain bikers, and other athletes, these daredevils prove that the sports world really has changed.

7. Only these "in-your-face" athletes are a small part of what is interesting about the changes taking place in sports today.

8. Occasionally, even fans of extreme sports know that the quest for adventure leads people into dangerous situations.

9. Environmentalists also point out unfortunately that in some remote wilderness areas, extreme sports are taking their toll on nature.

10. Probably, whether people love them or hate them, extreme sports will continue to inspire extreme reactions.

# PUNCTUATION

Name _____ Date _____ Section _____

For help with this exercise, see handbook section 11 in *Successful College Writing.*

## Exercise 11.1  End Punctuation

Correct any errors in the use of end punctuation marks in the following sentences. Some sentences may be correct as written.

**EXAMPLE:**

➤ No one knows what kind of undiscovered life forms exist at the bottom of the ocean~~?~~.

1. In some places, the ocean is more than seven miles deep!

2. Enormous pressure and complete darkness in the depths make it difficult for humans to discover what is down there?

3. When deep-sea fishing boats haul up their nets, they sometimes find creatures never before seen or prehistoric life forms that were believed to be extinct.

4. The sheer size of the ocean depths indicates that there may be many more species down there than are found on land!

5. Could there be millions of unknown species living in the deepest ocean trenches?

6. Scientists wonder what the implications of new species might be for human beings.

7. Is it also possible that the actions of humans are affecting life at the bottom of the sea.

8. Biologists who have recently measured the food supply on the ocean floor might be moved to exclaim, "It seems to be dwindling?"

9. Most of the food that reaches the bottom comes from near the surface, where there is light?

10. Warmer surface temperatures may be reducing the food supply at the bottom, and who has more influence on global warming than human beings.

For help with this exercise, see handbook section 12 in *Successful College Writing*.

## Exercise 12.1  Adding Commas

Add or omit commas as necessary in the following sentences. Some sentences may be correct as written.

**EXAMPLE:**

➤ Horse racing‚which has been a spectator sport for centuries‚still delights fans.

1. Breeders have long prized their swiftest, most graceful horses, and raced them.

2. Horse racing in the United States generally means either thoroughbred racing or harness racing.

3. Harness racehorses pull small lightweight vehicles, handled by a driver.

4. Harness racing falls into the two categories of trotting, and pacing.

5. The most famous event in harness racing the Hambletonian, is a mile-long trotting race.

6. Harness racing may be known mainly to enthusiasts but even people who appreciate very little about horse racing are familiar with thoroughbred racing.

7. Thoroughbred racehorses, unlike harness racehorses, carry a rider.

8. The best-known events in thoroughbred racing, the Kentucky Derby, the Preakness Stakes, and the Belmont Stakes, are the three races, that make up the Triple Crown.

9. All of the Triple Crown races which vary in length are for three-year-old horses.

10. In the twentieth century only eleven horses won thoroughbred racing's Triple Crown.

## Exercise 12.2  Working with Commas

Add or omit commas as necessary in the following sentences. Some sentences may be correct as written.

For help with this exercise, see handbook section 12 in *Successful College Writing*.

**EXAMPLE:**

➤ There are many theories/about the kinds of police work that are the most effective/at reducing crime.

1. Several years ago, many police departments ignored minor violations of the law, and concentrated on bigger crime problems.

2. Today, however, the "broken window" theory, is widely accepted.

3. According to this popular theory allowing broken windows to remain, unrepaired, leads to a loss of hope in a community.

4. Frequently, buildings that look neglected make neighbors feel that no one cares what goes on in the area.

5. Similarly, if petty crimes are ignored in a neighborhood people there may feel that larger crimes are acceptable as well.

6. Community policing is one result of the new emphasis on stopping "victimless" crimes such as loitering and panhandling.

7. But, can a police officer, walking a beat, really be more effective than a patrol car?

8. Some experts believe that police should be required to live in the communities, that they serve.

9. Police who live elsewhere may not understand the needs of the community, and they will certainly know less about the people living in the community.

10. Different methods of community policing may work in different areas but the goal should always be to keep communications open between the public and the police.

For help with
this exercise, see
handbook section
13 in *Successful
College Writing*.

## Exercise 13.1  Semicolons

Correct any errors in the use of semicolons in the following sentences. Some sentences may be correct as written.

**EXAMPLE:**

➤ The anti-Communist hysteria of the Cold War era marks one of the lowest points in American history;/when fear led to persecution of some citizens.

1. Many Americans think of the years after World War II as a golden era; a time before modern complexities made life more difficult.

2. Even without considering the quality of life at that time for women and minorities; an idyllic view of the mid-twentieth century ignores other issues.

3. The late 1940s and 1950s marked the height of the Cold War era; many Americans were frightened about what might happen in the future.

4. The Soviet Union, an ally of the United States during World War II, took control of the governments of neighboring countries, China, after a civil war, fell under Communist rule, and the Korean conflict, in which Americans were involved, seemed to prove that Communists wanted to take over as much land as possible.

5. Americans reacted to Communist activities elsewhere in the world, and part of their reaction included fear of communism at home.

6. Senator Joseph McCarthy may have shared this fear, he certainly capitalized on it to advance his political career.

7. In 1950, McCarthy announced that he had a list of Communists; who held positions in the U.S. State Department.

8. At about the same time, the House Un-American Activities Committee began investigating Hollywood; many stars were asked to testify about suspected Communists in the film industry.

9. Eventually, more than 150 film workers, including; performers, directors, and writers, were blacklisted by the Hollywood studios.

10. For the first half of the 1950s, anti-Communist leaders were very powerful in the United States; however, by 1955 McCarthy was in disgrace; and in 1957 the courts determined that membership in the Communist Party should no longer be a criminal offense in this country.

For help with this exercise, see handbook section 14 in *Successful College Writing*.

## Exercise 14.1  Colons

Correct any errors in the use of colons in the following sentences. Some sentences may be correct as written.

**EXAMPLE:**

➤ Near the end of the expedition, Scott and his men were⁄ cold, hungry, and exhausted.

1. In 1910, Robert Falcon Scott led his second expedition to Antarctica with two objectives to collect scientific data and to be the first humans at the South Pole.

2. The years before World War I were a heady time for: exploration of the frozen Antarctic continent.

3. The story of Scott's difficult journey continues to fascinate armchair adventurers: even though the expedition was, in many ways, a failure.

4. After arriving in Antarctica, Scott's scientists began their work, they collected specimens, surveyed the land, and recorded twelve volumes of data.

5. In 1911, Scott learned that the Norwegian explorer Roald Amundsen had decided to try to reach the South Pole as well.

6. Scott stuck to his original timetable for the South Pole journey, he did not want to engage in a race.

7. Scott and his men set out for the South Pole in the Antarctic summer of 1911: which is the winter season in the Northern Hemisphere.

8. In January 1912, Scott and the four companions who had traveled to the Pole with him were disappointed to learn that Amundsen's men had arrived a month earlier.

9. As they traveled back to their base camp, death took all five men Scott, Titus Oates, Edgar Evans, Henry Bowers, and Edward Wilson.

10. *Scott's Last Expedition: The Journals* records the explorer's last diary entry: "I do not think we can hope for any better things now. We shall stick it out to the end, but we are getting weaker, of course, and the end cannot be far. It seems a pity, but I do not think I can write more."

## Exercise 15.1  Quotation Marks

Correct any errors in the use of quotation marks in the following sentences.

For help with this exercise, see handbook section 15 in *Successful College Writing*.

**EXAMPLE:**

➤ Is Hamlet contemplating suicide when he says, "To be, or not to be, that is the question?"?

1. The film producer shouted excitedly, "Everyone loves Shakespeare because he used so many familiar quotations"!

2. "When we make movies based on Shakespeare plays", he added "we don't have to pay royalties to the writer."

3. Films based on Shakespeare plays try to reveal the relevance of his work to a "modern" audience.

4. Although Shakespeare lived four hundred years ago, his work is currently "in demand" in Hollywood.

5. "O," "10 things I hate about you," and "She's the Man" are just a few of Hollywood's modern interpretations of Shakespeare's plays.

6. The producer commented, "When I hear that a new film will be based on Shakespeare, I wonder, like Juliet, "What's in a name?" "

7. If the name Shakespeare were not involved, would filmmakers be as interested in the material?

8. Shakespeare's plays are frequently performed in theaters, too, and several young playwrights recently wrote works based on his "sonnets."

9. Hamlet, perhaps Shakespeare's most famous character, laments Alas, poor Yorick! I knew him, Horatio, a fellow of infinite jest, of most excellent fancy.

10. Othello, one of Shakespeare's most complex characters, laments that he "loved not wisely, but too well".

For help with this exercise, see handbook section 16 in *Successful College Writing*.

## Exercise 16.1 Ellipsis Marks

Shorten each quotation below by replacing the underlined portions with ellipsis marks, if appropriate. In some cases, an omission may be inappropriate.

**EXAMPLE:**

➤ "Don't tell me to get ready to die. ~~I know not what shall be~~. The only preparation I can make is by fulfilling my present duties" (Emerson 365).

1. "A writer <u>who keeps her audience in mind</u> cannot fail to be effective."

2. "<u>We hold these truths to be self-evident: that</u> all men are <u>created equal, that they are</u> endowed by their creator with certain inalienable rights, <u>that</u> among these are life, liberty, and the pursuit of happiness."

3. "<u>Even though he himself owned slaves,</u> Thomas Jefferson wanted the Declaration of Independence to say that all men were 'created independent.'"

4. Elizabeth Cady Stanton's "Declaration of Sentiments" announces, "<u>In entering upon the great work before us</u>, we anticipate no small amount of misconception, misrepresentation, and ridicule, <u>but we shall use every instrumentality within our power to effect our object</u>."

5. "Stanton's 'Declaration of Sentiments' was based <u>quite consciously</u> on the language Jefferson had used in the Declaration of Independence."

6. "<u>It may seem strange that</u> any men should dare to ask a just God's assistance in wringing their bread from the sweat of other men's faces; but let us judge not that we be not judged," Lincoln said in his second inaugural address.

7. "Allusions to the language of familiar literature, <u>such as the Bible or the Declaration of Independence</u>, can lend authority to a text that uses them well."

8. Lincoln went on, "Fondly do we hope — <u>fervently do we pray</u> — that this mighty scourge of war may speedily pass away."

9. Martin Luther King Jr. expressed the wish that his children would be judged "<u>not by the color of their skin, but</u> by the content of their character."

10. "Repetition of structure can be an effective rhetorical device. <u>This is true whether the work is intended for an audience of readers or listeners.</u>"

## Exercise 17.1 Apostrophes

Correct any errors in the use of apostrophes in the following sentences. Some sentences may be correct as written.

For help with this exercise, see handbook section 17 in *Successful College Writing.*

**EXAMPLE:**

➤ Some explorer's ideas about the ruins in Mashonaland were incorrect.

1. African chief's stories led a German explorer to the stone ruins in Mashonaland, now in Zimbabwe, in 1871.

2. The explorer, who's name was Karl Mauch, tried to find out who had built the once-great city.

3. The tribes nearby could not answer Mauches' question, but they knew gold had been found there.

4. The African's called the site *Zimbabwe.*

5. Mauch became convinced that the city was Ophir, the source of the gold brought back to King Solomon's Israel around 1000 B.C.E.

6. He thought perhaps the cities' builder was the Queen of Sheba.

7. An archeologists' findings later demonstrated that the city was about six hundred years old and that it had been built by African natives.

8. The Shona tribe probably built the first walls on the site, but it's more complex structures were added later by the Rozwi tribe.

9. The Rozwi probably erected the temple, which was inhabited by Rozwi ruler-priests until their empire's end in the 1830's.

10. The legends about the origins of the city persisted for a long time, perhaps because of white South Africans and Europeans' resistance to the idea that black Africans had built the impressive structures.

For help with this exercise, see handbook section 18 in *Successful College Writing.*

## Exercise 18.1 Parentheses and Brackets

Correct any errors in the use of parentheses or brackets in the following sentences.

**EXAMPLE:**

➤ The film poster announced, "The monster takes its revenge" [sic]."

1. Bad movies, (some of which are quite enjoyable to watch), often have a cult following.

2. Some films routinely make every critic's list of worst films (Usually, these movies are so bad they are funny.).

3. A few filmmakers [like Ed Wood] and movie companies [like American International Pictures] have acquired fame among fans of bad movies.

4. Roger Corman's American International Pictures [AIP] churned out innumerable inexpensive, quickly made films.

5. One Corman film, *Little Shop of Horrors,* (1960) was filmed in less than three days.

6. But the director Edward D. Wood Jr. [1924–1978] has a special place in the world of bad movies.

7. Wood gained new fame with Tim Burton's film biography, *Ed Wood,* (1994).

8. Like Corman's movies, Wood's were made very quickly, but Wood, (unlike Corman), thought he was making great films.

9. Wood's "masterpiece," *Plan 9 from Outer Space,* (Bela Lugosi's last film) is a science fiction and horror film with bad acting, dreadful writing, and laughable special effects.

10. Wood said that "*Plan 9* (was his) pride and joy."

## Exercise 21.1  Abbreviations

Correct any errors in the use of abbreviations in the following sentences.

For help with
this exercise, see
handbook section
21 in *Successful
College Writing.*

> **EXAMPLE:**
> *organizations*
> ➤ Humanitarian ~~orgs.~~ provide relief in disaster areas worldwide.
> ^

1. When disasters strike, victims count on international organizations like the Red Cross, Doctors without Borders, etc.

2. A Dr.'s help is often the most desperately needed form of aid.

3. People often offer canned goods and blankets, while major corps. receive tax benefits for donations of drugs and other medical supplies.

4. When Hurricane Mitch devastated Honduras, many U.S. cits. were quick to help.

5. An R.N. who is willing to travel to the disaster area can provide needed services.

6. For several years, volunteer doctors have tried to alleviate the AIDS crisis in Afr.

7. In some situations, e.g. during outbreaks of deadly diseases or in war-torn areas, medical personnel risk their own lives.

8. Doctors from the Atlanta, Ga.-based Centers for Disease Control travel the globe to isolate and study dangerous viruses.

9. The CDC doctors do not provide medical assistance in war zones, but other orgs. do.

10. In the aftermath of bloody fighting, a U.N. peacekeeping force may arrive to find intl. doctors already at work.

For help with
this exercise, see
handbook section
22 in *Successful
College Writing*.

## Exercise 22.1  Numbers

Correct any errors in the use of numbers in the following sentences.

**EXAMPLE:**

➤ The Beatles had more number <sub>one</sub> hits than any other group in pop history.

1. John Lennon, Paul McCartney, George Harrison, and Ringo Starr were 4 young men from Liverpool, England, who formed what would become the most popular rock band of all time.

2. On January twenty-five, 1964, the Beatles' first hit entered the U.S. charts.

3. The song "I Want to Hold Your Hand" spent seven weeks at number one and 14 weeks in the top 40.

4. Almost immediately, the Beatles began to attract 1000s of screaming fans everywhere they went.

5. Throughout the nineteen-sixties, the Beatles were the world's most popular group.

6. During the eight years of the Beatles' reign on the charts, they had more than forty three-minute pop hits.

7. By the 2nd half of the decade, the Beatles had stopped touring.

8. They performed live together for the last time on the roof of Three Savile Row, the headquarters of their doomed record company, Apple.

9. 150 employees worked for Apple, which eventually went bankrupt.

10. By no means did each Beatle earn twenty-five percent of the group's profits, for Lennon and McCartney wrote more than ninety percent of the songs.

## Exercise 23.1  Italics and Underlining

Correct any errors in the use of italics in the following sentences.

For help with this exercise, see handbook section 23 in *Successful College Writing*.

**EXAMPLE:**

➤ <u>Information overload</u>, a condition that makes people feel overwhelmed in the face of almost unlimited information, affects many Americans.

1. Americans today get their information from 60 Minutes, the New York Times, electronic sources, and thousands of other places.

2. Once, choices were limited: to find out about raising a child, for example, parents consulted Dr. Spock's book "Baby and Child Care."

3. Now, magazines like Parenting compete with the new edition of *Dr. Spock* and dozens of other titles.

4. Obscure information is more accessible than ever, so a fan of the song *Telstar* can find *The Joe Meek Story,* a full-length biography of its producer.

5. A student wanting to learn about the dead language called Old English could consult Web sites like the one maintained by *Georgetown University*.

6. It may no longer be possible for a single person to know all about, for example, *biology*.

7. Once, the term Renaissance man or Renaissance woman referred to a person well educated and talented in many subjects.

8. Leonardo da Vinci, the original Renaissance man, not only painted the "Mona Lisa" but also wrote botanical treatises and devised remarkable engineering plans.

9. Today, we do not expect the builder of the ocean liner Queen Elizabeth II to know other subjects.

10. A lifetime of study may lie behind a single article in the New England Journal of Medicine.

For help with
this exercise, see
handbook section
24 in *Successful
College Writing.*

## Exercise 24.1 Hyphens

Correct any errors in the use of hyphens in the following sentences.

**EXAMPLE:**

➤ Buying lottery/tickets is an extremely inefficient way to gain additional income.

1. Does buying lottery tickets and entering sweepstakes make a person selfemployed?

2. The odds of winning a major lottery prize are often over a million-to-one.

3. Yet many people, including desperately-poor ones who cannot afford the tickets, buy large numbers of them when the jackpot is high and the odds are worst.

4. A sensible approach to such sky high odds would be not to enter the lottery at all.

5. Sweepstakes are well-known to anyone with a mailbox.

6. Unlike lotteries, apparently-free sweepstakes do not require any cash investment other than the price of a stamp.

7. Yet many sweepstakes imply that buying a magazine-subscription or a product improves the chances of winning.

8. Some sweepstakes companies have been accused of trying to dupe customers who do not read the fine-print.

9. Some elderly people have thrown away their great grandchildren's inheritance, buying hundreds of products they don't need from sweepstakes advertisers.

10. The idea of getting rich with minimal work or investment is so strikingly-attractive that many people put logic aside and come up with the money.

## Exercise 25.1  Spelling

Correct any spelling errors in the following paragraph.

For help with this exercise, see handbook section 25 in *Successful College Writing*.

**EXAMPLE:**

➤ It sometimes ~~seams~~ *seems* as if every business ~~dicision~~ *decision* today has to go through a focus group.

    Focus groups consist of people selected to express there opinions about products rangeing from sneakers and gum to movies. Some times people who are supposed to be experts on a subject are selected. When companys test a new product, they choose people who might realisticly be expected to by it. If marketers are tring out a new soft drink, for example, they might ask teen agers for their advise. A company makeing a luxery car would be more inclined to seek the veiws of upper-middle-class buyers. On other ocasions, a focus group is picked at random. To find out how much consumors like a new TV show, a network might ask shoppers at a mall to watch an episode and discuss it with other participants. The network could than learn, not only what viewers like and dislike about the show, but also which groups are most likly to watch it. This information helps the network determine what changes to make in the show and what sponsers to approach. Of course, sense many people perfer the familiar, focus groups sometimes insure that tryed and true formulas ocurr again and again at the expense of new ideas.

Name _____  Date _____  Section _____

For help with
this exercise, see
handbook section
26 in *Successful
College Writing.*

## Exercise 26.1 Nouns and Articles

Correct any errors in the use of nouns or articles in the following sentences.

> **EXAMPLE:**
> ~~National~~ parks of the United States remind visitors of the great natural ~~beauties~~
> *The national*                                                                    *beauty*
> of this country.

1. The first American land set aside for a national public park was Yellowstone National Park, which was established in 1872 by a President Ulysses S. Grant.

2. Yellowstone National Park has not only the beautiful scenery but also the strange results of ancient volcanoes.

3. Underground lava left from the millions of years ago heats cold ground-water.

4. This heating results in hot springs, geysers, and the boiling muds.

5. Sequoia National Park, second national park established in the United States, is the home of many giant sequoia trees.

6. To the north of the Sequoia National Park is the third oldest national park, Yosemite National Park.

7. Like Sequoia National Park, Yosemite National Park offers the area of incredible beauty.

8. A waterfalls are found in some of our nation's oldest parks, such as Yosemite National Park and Niagara Reservation State Park.

9. Many other national parks have unusual natural formations; Denali National Park, for example, contains a highest mountain in North America.

10. A visitor who takes the time to see America's national parks will have a experience he or she will never forget.

## Exercise 26.2  Count and Noncount Nouns

In each sentence, circle the correct count or noncount noun in parentheses.

For help with this exercise, see handbook section 26 in *Successful College Writing.*

**EXAMPLE:**

➤  Arielle got her (nail, (nails)) manicured for the wedding.

1.  I plan to serve (shrimp, shrimps) at our party tomorrow night.

2.  When you go to the store later, please pick up two pints of (cream, creams).

3.  Please make the three (bed, beds) upstairs before you leave.

4.  Did someone dust the (furniture, furnitures) in the living room?

5.  The (smoke, smokes) from Paulie's cigar made me cough.

6.  Please put the (book, books) back on the shelves where they belong.

7.  I will sweep up the (sand, sands) in the front hall.

8.  Tell Daniel that he must put all of his (tool, tools) back in the garage.

9.  I don't want any of his (equipment, equipments) lying around when the guests arrive.

10.  Let's check yesterday's and today's (mail, mails) to see who is coming to the party.

For help with
this exercise, see
handbook section
27 in *Successful
College Writing*.

## Exercise 27.1 Verbs

Correct any errors in the use of the underlined verbs in the following sentences.
Some sentences may be correct as written.

**EXAMPLE:**

➤ Carlos Santana <u>have</u> some American radio hits with English lyrics and some with
Spanish lyrics.

*has had* (above "have", with caret ^)

1. As a young boy in Mexico, Carlos Santana learned <u>playing</u> the clarinet and
   violin.

2. From his early years, Carlos Santana never stopped <u>to play</u> instruments.

3. When Santana was fourteen, he <u>taked</u> up the guitar.

4. The Santana family <u>was moving</u> to San Francisco in 1962, when Carlos was
   fifteen.

5. By 1967, Santana <u>has formed</u> a band.

6. The Santana Blues Band <u>begun</u> to make a name in San Francisco clubs.

7. San Francisco in the late 1960s <u>had been</u> a center for new musical talent,
   and Santana's band attracted attention.

8. The promoters of the 1969 Woodstock Music Festival asked the band, now
   called Santana, <u>playing</u> at their three-day outdoor concert.

9. Carlos Santana, who <u>just turned</u> twenty-two, led his band through a long
   composition called "Soul Sacrifice."

10. The crowds <u>were</u> delighted, and Santana <u>became</u> a star.

## Exercise 27.2  Infinitives and Gerunds

For help with this exercise, see handbook section 27 in *Successful College Writing*.

For each of the following sentences, fill in the blank with the appropriate infinitive or gerund formed from the verb in parentheses.

**Example:**

➤ It is easy to understand foreign students' _____*being*_____ (be) confused about grades in American university classes.

1. Most U.S. professors prefer their students _____ (work) independently, but professors do offer help to students who need it.

2. University policies forbid _____ (share) answers to a test.

3. However, instructors often encourage their students _____ (collaborate) in teams on projects other than tests and papers.

4. Universities consider _____ (plagiarize) written work as grounds for expulsion.

5. Dishonest students may jeopardize their relationship with other students who resent their _____ (cheat).

6. Instructors expect students _____ (do) the work for a class even if the work is not graded.

7. Some teachers believe that not grading an assignment enables students _____ (judge) their own work.

8. If students want to improve their grades, professors often support students' _____ (work) with a tutor.

9. But most professors don't appreciate their students' _____ (ask) about grades on a test or paper in the middle of class.

10. Students who want class time to discuss grades risk _____ (anger) their professors.

For help with
this exercise, see
handbook section
27 in *Successful
College Writing*.

## Exercise 27.3  Modal Verbs

In the exercise below, circle the correct modal auxiliary.

**EXAMPLE:**

➤  May/(Would) you help me complete the assignment?

1.  It doesn't rain very often in Arizona, but today it looks like it (can/might).

2.  I know I (will/ought to) call my aunt on her birthday, but I always find an excuse.

3.  Sarah (should/must) study for her English exam, but she is happier spending time with her friends.

4.  John (can/would) be the best person to represent our class.

5.  Since the close presidential election of 2000, many people now believe they (could/should) vote in every election.

6.  All students (will/must) bring two pencils, a notebook, and a dictionary to class every day.

7.  (Would/May) you show me the way to the post office?

8.  I (could/should) not ask for more than my health, my family, and my job.

9.  Do you think they (could/can) come back tomorrow to finish the painting job?

10.  A dog (should/might) be a helpful companion for your disabled father.

## Exercise 28.1  The Prepositions *in, on,* and *at*

Fill in each blank with the correct preposition: *in, on,* or *at.*

For help with this exercise, see handbook section 28 in *Successful College Writing.*

**EXAMPLE:**

➤ Putting fresh vegetables __*in*__ a salad makes a tremendous difference.

1. For many people, a feature of modern life is eating food that comes _____ cans or boxes.

2. _____ dinnertime, the convenience of frozen and canned food is undeniable, but there is a trade-off.

3. Many Americans have grown dissatisfied with the convenience foods available _____ the supermarket.

4. Frequently, shoppers are willing to look harder for foods grown _____ local farms.

5. Both farmers and city dwellers benefit when agricultural products are available _____ urban areas.

6. Farmers get extra money _____ their pockets, and city people get delicious vegetables.

7. Why should rural dwellers be the only ones to enjoy an ear of sweet corn _____ a July day?

8. Farm products grown nearby also retain more vitamins than foods that have traveled long distances _____ a truck or train.

9. Decades ago, when most Americans sat _____ the dinner table, the foods they ate were likely to come from local growers.

10. _____ the United States today, regional foods and local produce are making a healthy comeback.

For help with
this exercise, see
handbook section
29 in *Successful
College Writing*.

## Exercise 29.1  Adjectives

Correct any errors in the use of adjectives in the following sentences. Some sentences may be correct as written.

**EXAMPLE:**

➤ ~~Brightly colored,~~ F , *brightly colored* fluffy quilts are great to have in the autumn and winter *cold* ~~cold~~
weather.

1. The three first quilts that I made were not very intricate.

2. My fourth quilt's pattern, however, comprised 2,000 two-inch squares of multicolored fabric.

3. I found inspiration for the pattern in a short magazine article about memory quilts.

4. The article said that the most best memory quilts don't have fabric new in them.

5. To make the squares for my memory quilt, I cut up my old son's shirts and boxer shorts.

6. He has many drawers full of clothing that he has outgrown.

7. Assembling a memory quilt from these items was an opportunity good for me to make space in his bureau and to practice my sewing.

8. It was also an opportunity good for me to preserve his memories childhood.

9. My son considers it a treasured heirloom.

10. He thought the wonderful quilt was an idea, and he now wants me to make one bigger.

## Exercise 30.1  Common Sentence Problems

Correct any common sentence problems in the following sentences.

For help with this exercise, see handbook section 30 in *Successful College Writing*.

**EXAMPLE:**

➤ Contagious diseases have frightened ‸throughout history *people around the* ‸ *world*.

*people around the world*

1. Many people once believed that the twentieth century would produce medical miracles would bring an end to infectious diseases.

2. Medical research had not made at the end of the twentieth century this wish a reality.

3. Vaccines removed from the list of childhood diseases some terrible illnesses, such as polio.

4. One dangerous disease completely disappeared in the twentieth century was smallpox.

5. However, a few laboratories can still provide to trusted researchers access to samples of the virus.

6. Ordinary people forgot about smallpox their fears, but other diseases soon took its place.

7. The AIDS epidemic struck in the 1980s many previously healthy young people.

8. AIDS proved that medical science could declare total victory never over disease.

9. In the same decade, other terrifying new viruses that their existence was until recently unknown, such as Ebola, raced through local populations.

10. Medicine today can reveal much more about diseases than people knew during medieval plagues, but not always can this knowledge save the lives of sick people.

For help with
this Exercise, see
handbook section
30 in *Successful
College Writing.*

## Exercise 30.2 Forming Negative Sentences

Rewrite each sentence in the space provided so that it correctly expresses a negative statement.

**EXAMPLE:**

➤   The president will veto the tax bill.

*The president will not veto the tax bill.* _____

1.   Speed limits are a good idea.

   _____

2.   Hector knows the baseball scores.

   _____

3.   He is a baseball fan.

   _____

4.   Olga understands the importance of math class.

   _____

5.   Medical careers are where math skills make the most difference.

   _____

6.   Conversation is acceptable in the library.

   _____

7.   Morning is the hardest time for Julia to concentrate.

   _____

8.   Young hunters can shoot safely.

   _____

9.   Marco always worries about the health of his relatives in Brazil.

   _____

10.  The high school may build a new gymnasium.

   _____

# ANSWERS TO EXERCISES

**Exercise P.1  Possible Answers** (page 1)

1. Given that America is not the only nation with a tradition of rich food, Americans are right to wonder why obesity is not as big a problem in other countries as it is here in America.
2. Studies show that many children who are patients in hospitals enjoy visits from trained pet therapists.
3. Though I didn't finish the race, running in the Boston Marathon taught me a lot about determination and friendship.
4. Effective
5. Because the convenience of the Internet allows people to browse more profiles faster, online dating is becoming popular as a more efficient way of meeting people.
6. Effective
7. Keeping up with the intimate details of movie stars' lives has become more important to some American teenagers than knowing the crucial details of American history.
8. One of the places where we can still find harmful stereotypes of African Americans, Native Americans, and Arabs is in Disney movies.
9. Like many other supposedly public places, national parks now charge fees that are far too high for the average visitor.
10. Effective

**Exercise P.2  Possible Answers** (page 3)

1. Most ordinary Americans, however, like their government, need to borrow money in order to survive economically.
2. Modern technology, however, has made it possible for many Americans to avoid the exercise that was once a part of daily life in this country.
3. Therefore, parents who want to give their child a head start should begin to play classical music for the child even before the baby's birth.

**Exercise P.3  Answers** (page 5)

1. (5) Interestingly, the word *bagatelle* can also refer to a short poem or piece of music.
2. (4) According to folklore, when observers see one of these "shooting stars," they should make a wish. (5) Vaporized matter from burned-out meteors adds about ten tons to the mass of the earth every day.
3. (3) Running a family farm has never been easy. (7) The expense of new harvesting machines, called combines, and the need to get the harvest in as quickly as possible are major reasons farmers hire custom cutters rather than doing the work themselves.

**Exercise P.4  Answers** (page 7)

1. One alternative to drugs for treating depression is the controversial Eye Movement Desensitization and Reprocessing or EMDR. This treatment is particularly useful for people who are depressed as a result of a traumatic event. ~~Prozac is also useful for treat-~~

ing depression. ~~For those who don't respond to Prozac, doctors often recommend Zoloft.~~ In an EMDR session, the therapist makes hand motions or flashes a light in front of the patient's face while he or she talks about an upsetting experience. ~~People who have experienced trauma often need a lot of support.~~ Many people have found this nontraditional therapy to be very helpful in processing their experiences, though no one knows for sure why EMDR works. ___*not unified*___

2. The advertisements that now appear before the movie are not effective because they only make moviegoers irritable. ~~Coke is one of the most frequently advertised products and one of the most recognized American brands. People often drink Coke or other soft drinks when they go to the movies.~~ Ads take away from the otherwise enjoyable experience of seeing a movie in the theater. These days, you have to sit through ten minutes of commercials before the previews start. ~~Advertisers also use product placement as a way to increase their product's visibility.~~ By the time the movie begins, you may already have been in your seat for half an hour. Because of this inconvenience, people may decide that it's worthwhile to wait for the DVD and skip the ads. Movie-theater owners would be wise to remember their paying audience and reconsider this partnership with advertisers.
___*not unified*___

3. Unified

4. One of America's most well-known and important court cases is the Scopes "Monkey Trial." ~~Students should learn their country's history at an early age. Knowing the past can help us predict the future.~~In 1925, John Scopes, a high school biology teacher, was charged with violating state law by teaching the theory of evolution to his students. He believed he was teaching an important scientific theory, but others believed that evolution contradicted the story of creation told in the Bible. The trial became famous because so many people had such strong feelings on both sides. It has also remained relevant because we haven't come to a definitive conclusion about which ideas students should or should not learn in school. ~~There are many old conflicts that remain unresolved. For instance, people have been arguing for decades over whether or not abortion should be legal.~~ ___*not unified*___

5. More animal shelters should adopt a "no kill" policy. Controlling the stray animal population by euthanizing is not the best solution. Killing unwanted pets solves the problem of overpopulation only temporarily, and it creates a bigger problem because it teaches people that animals are disposable. ~~Many people don't consider snakes, iguanas, and other reptiles as pets. When I was seven, I adopted a snake from our local shelter, and he turned out to be a wonderful pet.~~ We need to learn to be kinder and more responsible when it comes to animals. We need to have pets fixed and accept them even when they have special needs. ~~We need to accept humans with special needs as well.~~ Many of the animals in shelters are there because they were neglected or mistreated. If we change our own behavior, fewer animals will end up abused and unwanted. ___*not unified*___

6. Buying a house is not always a good investment. People who sell their houses after owning them for only a couple of years often lose money. ~~Spending money on a computer is not always a good investment either. Computers lose their value very quickly. Unless the buyer uses the computer for work, money spent on a computer is money lost.~~ People who don't buy enough insurance for their homes can lose money if there is a fire, flood, or other disaster. Houses also require a lot of maintenance. When people sell their houses,

often they find it difficult to make back the money they spent fixing up the house. Sometimes people are better off investing their money in something that does not cost so much. _not unified_

7. Unified

8. Hilary Swank is a positive role model for young actresses. ~~Jennifer Lopez is a good role model for future dancers and singers. Many girls look up to their mothers as well.~~ Unlike many successful women in the movie industry, Swank is not afraid to challenge herself when choosing roles. In both *Boys Don't Cry* and *Million Dollar Baby,* Swank focuses not on looking pretty but on inhabiting her characters and their difficult lives. Her determination and willingness to take these risks may come in part from her background. She was not born into a rich or privileged family and, like some of the characters she plays, she has had to work very hard to achieve her goals. ~~Many famous people have rough starts. Jennifer Lopez did not come from a rich family.~~ It's important for young girls to see a successful movie star who has dedication, integrity, and a real love of acting. _not unified_

## Exercise P.5 Possible Revisions (page 11)

1. A family gathering is supposed to fill us with a joyful sense of belonging, but it may not. Getting together for a family event, such as Thanksgiving dinner, can produce anxiety, anger, or depression just as often as it results in a warm, satisfied glow. People who are thrown together because they are related — by blood or by marriage — don't necessarily understand or like each other especially well. When relatives and in-laws get together, there are bound to be members of the group who don't get along. In my family, for example, my brother Philip and my aunt Julia are likely to get into an argument about some topic. Because family members are supposed to love each other, Philip and Julia usually try to talk with each other politely, never going into much depth or discussing dangerous topics such as politics, but the strain of trying to be nice can make them tense. And if they both have a few beers, the two of them don't even really try to chat any longer; they just glare at one another from their respective corners of the long dining-room table. Finally, Philip makes a sarcastic remark, Julia spits back a furious reply, and the rest of us feel embarrassed.

2. A movie can't be good unless all of the pieces — from the directing and screenwriting to the casting and music — come together successfully. I recently saw *Titanic* and thought that the concept and special effects were great, but the script was padded with laughable lines and two completely unnecessary gunfights. The script isn't always the problem; in *She's Gotta Have It,* for example, there was some fine writing, but the lead actress, Tracy Camilla Johns, never let the audience forget she was only playing a role. In contrast, Sean Penn and Christopher Walken were convincing as father and son in *At Close Range,* but the events in that movie happened so slowly that I wondered what the director, James Foley, was thinking. Even if everything else is on target, overbearing music can ruin a good scene, as in parts of *Saving Private Ryan,* where composer John Williams doesn't seem to trust the audience to know what to feel. With so many variables, it's a wonder that any good movies exist. They do, of course; *Rushmore* and *Big Night* are just two examples of recent films whose witty scripts, fine acting, crisp pace, and mood-enhancing music made audiences feel that everything about them was right.

3.  Children should have a dog or cat as soon as they are old enough to play gently with it and avoid hurting it. Feeding and cleaning up after a pet is a good experience for any child. If parents are firm with their children and don't do their animal-care chores for them, the children will learn how to behave responsibly; it's hard to ignore or forget a beloved dog waiting for his little owner to feed and walk him. Additionally, having a pet can teach children about loving and protecting a creature weaker than themselves; any child who has ever held a contented, purring cat will find it very hard to be cruel to any animal. Responsibility and empathy are valuable lessons for children to learn and can help them grow into humane, decent adults. Finally, having a dog or cat can be a reward in itself—the animal returns affection and can actually make a child's life happier. At times, such as when parents or friends have disappointed a child, the family dog or cat will be a steadfast companion. Most adults who had a pet in childhood have wonderful memories of a much-loved Fido or Fluffy.

### Exercise P.6  Answers (page 12)

1.  Underdeveloped
2.  Underdeveloped
3.  Well developed
4.  Underdeveloped
5.  Well developed
6.  Underdeveloped
7.  Underdeveloped
8.  Underdeveloped

### Exercise P.7  Possible Revisions (page 17)

1.  The French may still have the international reputation of being the people most interested in gourmet food, **but** Americans are quickly gaining **gastronomical ground. Once,** "American food" meant fast foods like hamburgers and hot dogs, **and in fact,** people around the world still associate these foods with American culture. **That perception is not entirely accurate now**: U.S. food lovers may seek out the best burgers, fries, and barbecue foods, **but** they also want to sample foods from ethnic cultures within the United States and **from** other countries. **Today,** people want the best of what American produce has to offer and will go far to find fresh, local ingredients that are expertly prepared.

2.  Modern conceptions of timekeeping owe a lot to the ancient Babylonians. **They** gave people today the twelve-month year, the twenty-four-hour day, the sixty-minute hour, and the sixty-second minute. The number *twelve* was significant to the **Babylonian culture because the people** noticed that there were usually twelve full moons in a year. **Therefore**, the Babylonian calendar contained twelve months of thirty days each. **Because** five days were left over each year, every six years they had to add an extra month to the year. **Continuing to emphasize the mystical number *twelve,* the Babylonians** divided the day and night into twelve hours each. **In addition to *twelve,*** the number *sixty* was important to **this culture because it** can be evenly divided by many integers—two, three, four, five, six, ten, twelve, fifteen, twenty, and thirty. **Consequently, Babylonian time** divided

each hour into sixty minutes and each minute into sixty seconds. **Later**, the Romans changed the length of some Babylonian months from thirty to thirty-one or twenty-eight days, **but** the Babylonians' other time measurements survive to this day.

3. The Restoration period in England, which began with the return of the monarchy in 1660, was marked by the kind of public behavior on the part of aristocrats and courtiers that would still provoke a shocked reaction today. **The Restoration king**, Charles II, served as the model of moral—or immoral—behavior for members of his court. **Charles had** no children by his wife, **but** he had a large number of children by his several mistresses. **Following the king's example**, young male courtiers boasted of numerous love affairs. **To please these aristocrats**, court poets and dramatists composed bawdy, amoral literary works. Many **of these works** contained words and suggestions that even modern newspapers would not print. **During the Restoration**, the public loved to attend performances of plays **even though** simply being seen at a theater could give a person a questionable reputation. The clergy and other representatives of moral authority protested the literary, theatrical, and personal misbehavior of the aristocrats. **Eventually**, bawdiness became less fashionable, **and** a much more conservative age followed the Restoration.

### Exercise P.8 Answers (page 19)

| | |
|---|---|
| **Title** | **More Than Just a Place to Sleep** |
| **Introduction** | *Thesis:* Though it requires some preparation and adaptability, staying at a traditional Japanese hotel, or *ryokan*, is an enjoyable and worthwhile way for a Western visitor to learn about Japanese culture. |

**Body Paragraph 1**  Finding a *ryokan*
- locate Web sites that list *ryokan*s (6)
- determine your price range
- decide how formal or informal a *ryokan* you'd like (2)
- make advance reservations

**Body Paragraph 2**  Apparel etiquette in a *ryokan*
- take off your shoes when you enter the *ryokan* and put on slippers
- take off the slippers when walking on the tatami mats (3)
- wear *geta* (wooden clogs) if you stroll around the *ryokan* grounds
- wear your *yukata* (robe provided by the *ryokan*) when in the *ryokan* (4)
- *yukatas* should be worn left side over right; right side over left is for funerals (7)
- wear a *tanzen* (outer robe) over your *yukata* if you get cold

**Body Paragraph 3**  Japanese bath etiquette
- Japanese often bathe before dinner
- in changing room, put *yukata* in basket provided
- wash yourself in the bathing area using shower or basin before entering the public bath (9)
- do not drain the water from the tub when finished
- dry yourself thoroughly before returning to the changing room (8)

**Body Paragraph 4**    Engaging with your host or hosts
- learn a few key phrases in Japanese
- ask about the building and garden
- ask about the best sights to see in their town (5)

**Body Paragraph 5**    A day in the life of a different culture
- be willing to try unusual breakfast foods, like cold squid and miso soup (1)
- enjoy the serenity of life without television
- try meditating
- adjust to the firmness of a futon mattress (10)

**Conclusion**    While staying in a familiar Western-style hotel might feel easier, after a night or two in a *ryokan,* you'll find yourself more mindful of Japanese culture and traditions, and remarkably refreshed.

## Exercise E.1  Possible Answers (page 21)

1. American parents choose carefully when naming their children.
2. Comparing popular names of today and of the past shows how much our ideas about naming children have changed.
3. Girls' names have changed the most.
4. Forty years ago, most baby girls received traditional names rather than unusual ones.
5. Some of the older names gradually became less popular, and newer names, like Jennifer, now a perennial favorite, took their place.
6. Today, parents often give their daughters names that were once considered masculine, like Sidney or Taylor.
7. Some parents try to make their daughters' names seem unusual by spelling a traditional name in a nontraditional way.
8. Boys' names, however, have not changed as noticeably.
9. For decades the most popular boys' name has been Michael.
10. Perhaps, as the results of a recent poll suggest, parents think having an unusual name helps girls and harms boys.

## Exercise E.2  Possible Answers (page 22)

1. Nicotine, which is an addictive drug, is an ingredient in cigarettes.
2. No smoker sets out to become addicted to cigarettes, but most people have difficulty stopping once they start smoking.
3. Movies can affect young people profoundly; they often portray smokers as glamorous and sexy.
4. Many thirty-year-old people who do not smoke are unlikely to begin smoking.
5. The tobacco companies need new customers, and they are more apt to find such customers among the younger generations.
6. When some teenagers take up smoking, they don't consider the possible consequences.
7. The Joe Camel cartoon advertisements were controversial because cartoons often appeal to children.

8. The Joe Camel advertising campaign was withdrawn, and new restrictions have been placed on tobacco ads.

9. Smoking can be unsightly and unhealthy, but it is legal.

10. The number of lawsuits against tobacco companies has risen recently; families have argued that tobacco companies are to blame for the deaths of their loved ones.

## Exercise E.3 Possible Answers (page 23)

1. In the nineteenth century, criminal tendencies were mistakenly thought to be related to physical traits.

2. Phrenologists, who studied bumps on the skull, mapped the human head for anti-social protrusions.

3. They hoped that they could identify potential criminals before crimes occurred.

4. Carefully recording their findings, other researchers, followers of a pseudoscience called craniometry, measured the proportions of the human head.

5. Using measurements of skull circumference, craniometrists inferred conclusions about brain size and intelligence as well as criminality.

6. From the beginning, these scientists' studies were fatally flawed because they found what they expected to find.

7. Since these "sciences" fell out of favor in the mid-twentieth century, researchers have been focusing on psychology as a means of understanding criminal actions.

8. The debate over which influence is stronger, heredity or environment, continues among social scientists.

9. One of the key controversies among scientists, the issue may never be resolved to everyone's satisfaction.

10. In scientific inquiry, however, important questions generate useful research as well as theories that are later discredited.

## Exercise E.4 Answers (page 25)

1. The United States uses large amounts of energy, **depends** heavily on oil, and imports much of that oil.

2. Burning oil for energy pollutes the air, destroys an irreplaceable commodity, and **wastes** resources.

3. During the 1970s, an embargo made oil expensive and **difficult** to get.

4. The oil crisis led to a wider interest in alternative energy sources that would be renewable, environmentally sound, and **less expensive** than oil.

5. Some new homes used solar heating, although it was expensive to install and still relatively untested.

6. Many Americans expected electric cars to be perfected and widely available by the end of the twentieth century.

7. Instead, the embargo ended, the cost of oil dropped, and gasoline prices **declined**.

8. At the same time, money to invent alternative energy technologies, to develop new products, and **to market** the products dried up.

9. Scientists and **environmentalists** who study the environment hope that there will be plentiful renewable energy sources someday.

10. It would be better to have alternative energy possibilities soon than **to wait** for the world's oil reserves to run dry.

### Exercise E.5  Possible Answers (page 26)

1. Annual "Fashion Week" events in American and European cities draw big crowds.

2. Photographers, journalists, models, and celebrities attend shows by new and established designers.

3. Many people in the audience show off their model-thin bodies and photogenic faces.

4. Often, *haute couture* shows with their expensive, trend-setting fashions entice the largest numbers of eager spectators.

5. Designers do not expect ordinary people to wear *haute couture* garments.

6. Designers frequently consider their *haute couture* creations to be works of art rather than mere outfits.

7. Only runway models can wear such clothing in public.

8. Other people attract ridicule in *haute couture* clothes.

9. Dressers can drape clothes more easily on models who have very thin bodies.

10. The spectacle impresses some people more than the clothes do.

### Exercise E.6  Possible Answers (page 27)

Americans have recently been **forced to accept** the fact that anorexia nervosa, a disease of self-starvation, is becoming more widespread. Anorexia sufferers are overwhelmingly made up of teenage girls and young women. Most of them are white and come from middle-class or upper-class families. They are also usually **intelligent**. They seem to other people to have **nearly** every advantage. Their families and **friends** ordinarily have a **difficult** time comprehending why they will not eat. Because anorexia is a psychological disorder, the sufferers themselves may not **understand** what caused the onset of their illness. Anorexics have a **distorted** body image. They often believe they are **extremely** overweight unless they are dangerously **thin**. The disease is notoriously difficult to treat, even if the patient tries to **cooperate with** her doctors.

### Exercise E.7  Possible Answers (page 28)

1. Every year, almost all college-bound high school juniors take one or more college admissions tests.

2. A high test score can help a student gain admission to a prestigious college.

3. Test-preparation courses, which give students practice exams to measure their progress, are becoming popular.

4. These courses can cost hundreds of dollars.

5. Educators disagree about whether test-preparation courses actually help students prepare for the exam and for college work.

6. Many students who take a standardized test before and after a test-preparation course show at least some improvement in their scores after the course.

7. The amount of improvement may be only a few percentage points.

8. Opponents of the courses argue that by taking them, wealthy students can, in effect, buy a better score.

9. Others say that the scores of students who take test-preparation courses are not significantly higher than the scores of students who don't.

10. Many worried parents continue to pay for test preparation, reasoning that it can't hurt their children's chances.

### Exercise E.8 Possible Answers (page 29)

1. For generations, women were considered to be spun-glass angels too fragile for sports.

2. Many people thought that women would die like a butterfly in a whirlwind if they were too physically active.

3. Even though these mistaken beliefs were widespread, women athletes have moved forward, hurdling over all obstacles.

4. Individual women athletes, like the track and golf star Babe Didrikson Zaharias, had to be as strong as a well-toned muscle.

5. During World War II, a women's baseball league drew spectators like bees to a field of poppies when a shortage of male players depleted men's teams.

6. The end of the war drained the blood from the women's league.

7. The American women's movement of the 1970s was the beginning of a new season for women in sports.

8. A "battle of the sexes" took place in tennis during that decade, when Billie Jean King, a star female player, made Bobby Riggs, an avowed "male chauvinist" who had challenged her, look as weak as a newborn baby's grip.

9. In the following decades, some individual women became sports heroes, like Florence Griffith Joyner, who could run like a cheetah.

10. Finally, in the 1990s, the popularity of women's basketball and soccer spread like the "wave" in a packed stadium.

### Exercise E.9 Possible Answers (page 30)

1. The treatment of mental illness has troubled societies throughout history.

2. A thousand years ago, observers thought mental disturbance proved that the sufferer was possessed by demons.

3. Many mentally ill people died in the course of treatment for demonic possession.

4. Belief in demonic possession eventually decreased in much of the world.

5. Instead, doctors and others classified mental illness as a kind of disease.

6. Sufferers were frequently confined and, often, forgotten.

7. Officials decided that mentally ill people were antisocial, not sick.

8. Most healthy people rarely considered the mentally ill.

9. In the nineteenth century, a reformer, Dorothea Dix, investigated the treatment of the mentally ill in Massachusetts.

10. Her report shocked people so much that Massachusetts, and soon other states, legislated humane treatment for sufferers of mental illness.

### Exercise 1.1  Answers (page 31)

1. Verb
2. Noun
3. Verb
4. Noun
5. Pronoun
6. Verb
7. Noun
8. Pronoun
9. Verb
10. Noun

### Exercise 1.2  Answers (page 32)

1. Parents in the early twentieth century **were** warned that detective magazines could warp children's minds.
2. Pulp fiction about crime did indeed **become** rather lurid.
3. Correct
4. Many scholars have **given** Edgar Allan Poe credit for being the first author to write detective fiction in English.
5. Correct
6. Correct
7. Correct
8. Arthur Conan Doyle, the creator of Holmes and Watson, **was** amazed at the popularity of his fictional characters.
9. Correct
10. While not all detective stories are worthy of serious study, the best ones are **considered** by scholars to be very rewarding.

### Exercise 1.3  Answers (page 33)

1. Simple past
2. Past progressive
3. Present perfect
4. Past perfect
5. Simple present
6. Simple future
7. Past perfect
8. Past perfect progressive
9. Future progressive

10. Simple future

**Exercise 1.4 Answers** (page 34)

1. Subjunctive
2. Indicative
3. Indicative
4. Subjunctive
5. Imperative
6. Indicative
7. Subjunctive
8. Indicative
9. Indicative
10. Indicative

**Exercise 1.5 Answers** (page 35)

1. Adverb
2. Adjective
3. Adjective
4. Adjective
5. Adverb
6. Adjective
7. Adjective
8. Adverb
9. Adjective
10. Adverb

**Exercise 1.6 Answers** (page 36)

1. Preposition
2. Preposition
3. Conjunction
4. Preposition
5. Conjunction
6. Conjunction
7. Preposition
8. Conjunction
9. Conjunction
10. Preposition

**Exercise 2.1 Answers** (page 37)

1. Complete subject

2. Simple subject

3. Complete predicate

4. Complete predicate

5. Complete subject

6. Simple predicate

7. Simple predicate

8. Complete predicate

9. Simple subject

10. Simple predicate

## Exercise 2.2 Answers (page 38)

1. Subject complement

2. Object complement

3. Direct object

4. Subject complement

5. Direct object

6. Direct object

7. Object complement

8. Indirect object

9. Indirect object

10. Subject complement

## Exercise 2.3 Answers (page 39)

1. Appositive phrase

2. Prepositional phrase

3. Verbal phrase

4. Verbal phrase

5. Absolute phrase

6. Appositive phrase

7. Absolute phrase

8. Prepositional phrase

9. Verbal phrase

10. Appositive phrase

## Exercise 2.4 Answers (page 40)

1. Many superstitions date from classical or medieval times, <u>when belief in witchcraft was widespread</u>.

2. Superstitions were a way for people to explain <u>whatever threatened them</u>.

3. <u>Because cats were believed to be witches in disguise</u>, the fear of a black cat crossing one's path came about.

4. Walking under ladders has also long been considered unlucky; this superstition may survive <u>because it protects pedestrians from falling objects</u>.

5. Some people attribute to the Christian story of the Last Supper, <u>where thirteen people were present</u>, the origins of the superstitious fear of the number thirteen.

6. <u>Wherever it began</u>, fear of the number thirteen, or triskaidekaphobia, is still prevalent enough for many tall modern buildings not to have a thirteenth floor.

7. Early Romans believed <u>that sneezing was a sign of the plague</u>, so they feared it.

8. The method <u>they invented</u> to protect a sneezer was to say, "God bless you."

9. In the United States today, it is common to say "God bless you" — or "Gesundheit," <u>which is German for "health"</u> — following a sneeze.

10. Superstitions from the past may seem silly today, but <u>who knows what strange customs of the present will be ridiculed in the future</u>?

## Exercise 2.5  Answers (page 41)

1. Simple
2. Complex
3. Simple
4. Compound
5. Complex
6. Complex
7. Simple
8. Compound
9. Simple
10. Compound-complex

## Exercise 3.1  Possible Answers (page 42)

1. There are older and more valuable manuscripts than the Voynich.

2. However, there is none more mysterious. The Voynich is still puzzling scholars many years after its discovery.

3. This manuscript was written in a code. So far, no one has been able to solve it.

4. Because the origins of the manuscript are unclear, the puzzle is doubly difficult.

5. No one knows what country it came from.

6. Therefore, it is very hard to determine the language the code represents. This makes decoding it even more troublesome.

7. Correct

8. The writing does not resemble any letters that can be traced to a known alphabet.

9. The manuscript contains many beautiful illustrations. It depicts plants, people, and other seemingly unrelated images.

10. The Voynich manuscript is such an intriguing mystery that some scholars might actually be disappointed to learn all of its secrets.

### Exercise 4.1  Possible Answers (page 43)

1. Mae West began as a child star. The career of "Baby Mae" took off when she performed at a local Brooklyn theater's amateur night.
2. At the age of nineteen, West began performing on Broadway; she shocked audiences in 1911.
3. The voluptuous West became known for her suggestive clothing and even more famous for her suggestive wisecracks.
4. Attending black jazz clubs had introduced her to a new dance movement. She performed this "shimmy" on Broadway, and it became a trademark for her.
5. West was not satisfied for long with the theatrical roles she was offered; writing her own plays was one way to find good parts.
6. In 1925, she wrote a play called *Sex,* but no producer she contacted would bring it to the stage.
7. The following year, when West produced the play herself, advertisements for *Sex* were banned.
8. Nevertheless, the show played for nine months until it was closed down by the Society for the Suppression of Vice. West was arrested and spent eight days in jail.
9. In the 1930s and 1940s, Mae West took her naughty humor to Hollywood. While there she made a series of hit films and often wrote her own screenplays.
10. West made her final films in the 1970s. By that time Americans found her less scandalous, but her name was still a household word.

### Exercise 5.1  Answers (page 44)

1. The festival called "Juneteenth," which people once recognized only in a few southern areas of the United States, **is** now much more widespread.
2. Correct
3. The surrender of the Confederate States **was** made official at Appomattox Courthouse on April 9, 1865.
4. From that day on, the Confederacy and the Union **were** again a single country.
5. Neither the northern states nor the southern states **were** now legally able to permit slave-owning, which had been officially outlawed in the United States several years earlier.
6. Correct
7. The story from those long-ago days **goes** that in Texas, slave owners murdered the messengers bringing word of emancipation.
8. Not until June 19, 1865, **was** the news able to reach the last group of Texas slaves.
9. Correct
10. Today, people celebrating Juneteenth **attend** concerts, films, and other cultural events.

### Exercise 6.1  Answers (page 45)

1. The horrors of World War I **convinced** some artists that European society had to change radically.

2. Their reaction at first **consisted** of musical and performance events they called the Cabaret Voltaire.

3. Soon, however, the most influential members of the group **began** to focus on visual art.

4. **The artists chose** the name *Dada* at random.

5. They rejected older artistic traditions, including avant-garde ideas that **had** recently **become** popular.

6. Instead, the Dadaists **challenged** the whole concept of art.

7. Before the Dada movement **ended** in 1923, several of the artists had experimented with random arrangements of materials.

8. Sometimes they chose the material they **used** from items discarded by other people.

9. One artist, Marcel Duchamp, even **set** up ordinary objects at art shows, claiming that the act of choosing the objects made them art.

10. Dada was a rebellion, not an attempt to build a new tradition, so no identifiable stylistic legacy of the movement **remains** today.

## Exercise 7.1 Possible Answers (page 46)

1. Many political analysts say that public distrust of the U.S. government began with Watergate.

2. That scandal's continuing legacy may make Watergate one of the most influential American events of the twentieth century.

3. Since the early 1970s, political scandals have rarely interested Americans; the scandals often seem to have very little effect.

4. Journalists provided the American people with a lot of information about the Iran-Contra hearings, but the public could not have cared less.

5. Could the indifference of most people have been the result of post–Watergate trauma?

6. If Americans expect politicians to be corrupt, government scandals will not surprise or even interest the public.

7. Ironically, the media's coverage of scandals seems to have made the public suspicious of journalists as well.

8. Cynicism about political and journalistic motives, which can spread contagiously, leads to apathy.

9. Many people are so apathetic that they refuse to vote.

10. If people do not believe that they can make a difference in the political process, the country becomes less democratic.

## Exercise 7.2 Answers (page 47)

1. Meteorology has made many advances in the past few decades, but **it** still cannot answer a number of questions about tornados.

2. Every tornado has **its** own unique characteristics.

3. Correct

4. An F4 tornado or an F5 tornado can destroy everything in **its** path.

5. Scientists cannot predict precisely how strong any tornado will be before **it** happens.
6. One reason why meteorologists find it difficult to predict tornados is **their** many possible causes.
7. Tornados can form due to wind flow patterns, or **they** might be caused by other factors such as temperature, moisture, instability, and lift.
8. Correct
9. Either a few extra minutes of warning or more information about a storm's power would prove **its** effectiveness in saving lives.
10. People who live in a tornado zone should always know where **their** nearest safe area is.

## Exercise 7.3 Answers (page 48)

1. **We** residents of the United States are considered by much of the rest of the world to be an unusually violent people.
2. Many researchers have debated **their** theories about violent behavior in this country.
3. Did the popular myth of the "Wild West" influence **us** and our ancestors?
4. Other industrialized nations and **we** have very different policies concerning guns.
5. Correct
6. Violence and justice are so intertwined for many Americans that disagreements between other people and **them** can erupt into fights.
7. Correct
8. There are defenders of violent films, TV shows, and video games **who** claim that entertainment reflects our tastes rather than influencing them.
9. Correct
10. Sometimes it seems that our worst enemies are **we**.

## Exercise 8.1 Possible Answers (page 49)

1. West African villages have strong oral traditions in which parents and grandparents tell the younger people stories.
2. Before the Revolutionary War, slave traders forced ancestors of the people from those villages to come to the United States.
3. In their difficult new situation in this country, the Africans adapted their stories so that people could learn from them.
4. Although different stories had different messages, one kind of character came up over and over again.
5. The character is cunning and clever; he is a "trickster."
6. The stories about Br'er Rabbit are good examples of folktales whose hero is a trickster.
7. Many of the other animals want to eat Br'er Rabbit, who has only his wits to protect him.
8. Yet in every story, Br'er Rabbit not only escapes but he makes his enemies appear foolish as well.
9. Trickster characters like Br'er Rabbit showed slaves who heard these stories that they, too, could triumph by using cleverness when foes surrounded them.

10. Today, folklorists are exploring how early African Americans encouraged each other by telling stories of tricksters outsmarting powerful enemies.

## Exercise 8.2  Possible Answers (page 50)

1. Most people think falsehoods are easy to spot.
2. They think that nonverbal signals show when someone is lying.
3. These signals, such as avoiding eye contact or hesitating before answering a question, are habits of truthful people as well.
4. Liars are hard to identify because no single trait always proves that a person is lying.
5. One problem with lie detection is that truthful people who are afraid they will not be believed may act suspiciously.
6. A few people are unusually good at identifying liars.
7. However, perhaps because these people are attuned to deceitful behavior, they are not especially good at identifying truth-tellers.
8. A stranger's lies may be easier to detect than a loved one's.
9. The better someone knows and likes another person, the more difficult it seems to be to spot his or her lies.
10. Finding it hard to believe that one's friends would try to deceive one is an understandable human characteristic.

## Exercise 9.1  Possible Answers (page 51)

1. Many people go to a lot of trouble to look **attractive**.
2. In the United States, no one thinks a woman wearing high heels is dressed **strangely**.
3. Many Americans even go to **really** extreme lengths, such as having surgery, to be beautiful.
4. People can see the strangeness of beauty rituals **more clearly** if the rituals are unfamiliar.
5. For example, in China in past centuries, beautiful women had to have **tiny** feet.
6. To achieve this goal, families bound their daughters' feet so **tightly** that the feet could not grow.
7. Subcultures within the United States also have their own standards of beauty that may seem **odd** to people who are not part of the subculture.
8. For many young Americans, tattoos and body piercing were the **trendiest** fashion statements of the 1990s.
9. They might have argued that such beautification was no **more unusual** than plucking out one's eyebrows.
10. Parents, however, often felt **vast** relief if their children reached adulthood without tattoos.

## Exercise 10.1  Possible Answers (page 52)

1. Recently, several sports that no one had heard of thirty years ago have gained popularity.

2. With a name that suggests their dangerous allure, extreme sports are attracting members of Generation X.

3. These "Generation X" games, which include snowboarding and sky-surfing, often involve going to inaccessible places.

4. Snow activities that can be done on remote mountaintops are especially popular.

5. Some of these sports, such as freestyle skiing and snowboarding, have become so widely accepted that participants can now compete in the Olympics.

6. Gasping at the antics of snowboarders, mountain bikers, and other athletes, fans can see that the sports world really has changed.

7. These "in-your-face" athletes are only a small part of what is interesting about the changes taking place in sports today.

8. Even fans of extreme sports know that the quest for adventure occasionally leads people into dangerous situations.

9. Environmentalists also point out that in some remote wilderness areas, extreme sports are unfortunately taking their toll on nature.

10. Whether people love them or hate them, extreme sports will probably continue to inspire extreme reactions.

### Exercise 11.1  Answers (page 53)

1. In some places, the ocean is more than seven miles deep.

2. Enormous pressure and complete darkness in the depths make it difficult for humans to discover what is down there.

3. Correct

4. The sheer size of the ocean depths indicates that there may be many more species down there than are found on land.

5. Correct

6. Correct

7. Is it also possible that the actions of humans are affecting life at the bottom of the sea?

8. Biologists who have recently measured the food supply on the ocean floor might be moved to exclaim, "It seems to be dwindling!"

9. Most of the food that reaches the bottom comes from near the surface, where there is light.

10. Warmer surface temperatures may be reducing the food supply at the bottom, and who has more influence on global warming than human beings?

### Exercise 12.1  Answers (page 54)

1. Breeders have long prized their swiftest, most graceful horses and raced them.

2. Correct

3. Harness racehorses pull small, lightweight vehicles handled by a driver.

4. Harness racing falls into the two categories of trotting and pacing.

5. The most famous event in harness racing, the Hambletonian, is a mile-long trotting race.

6. Harness racing may be known mainly to enthusiasts, but even people who appreciate very little about horse racing are familiar with thoroughbred racing.

7. Correct

8. The best-known events in thoroughbred racing, the Kentucky Derby, the Preakness Stakes, and the Belmont Stakes, are the three races that make up the Triple Crown.

9. All of the Triple Crown races, which vary in length, are for three-year-old horses.

10. In the twentieth century, only eleven horses won thoroughbred racing's Triple Crown.

### Exercise 12.2 Answers (page 55)

1. Several years ago, many police departments ignored minor violations of the law and concentrated on bigger crime problems.

2. Today, however, the "broken window" theory is widely accepted.

3. According to this popular theory, allowing broken windows to remain unrepaired leads to a loss of hope in a community.

4. Correct

5. Similarly, if petty crimes are ignored in a neighborhood, people there may feel that larger crimes are acceptable as well.

6. Correct

7. But can a police officer walking a beat really be more effective than a patrol car?

8. Some experts believe that police should be required to live in the communities that they serve.

9. Correct

10. Different methods of community policing may work in different areas, but the goal should always be to keep communications open between the public and the police.

### Exercise 13.1 Answers (page 56)

1. Many Americans think of the years after World War II as a golden era, a time before modern complexities made life more difficult.

2. Even without considering the quality of life at that time for women and minorities, an idyllic view of the mid-twentieth century ignores other issues.

3. Correct

4. The Soviet Union, an ally of the United States during World War II, took control of the governments of neighboring countries; China, after a civil war, fell under Communist rule; and the Korean conflict, in which Americans were involved, seemed to prove that Communists wanted to take over as much land as possible.

5. Correct

6. Senator Joseph McCarthy may have shared this fear; he certainly capitalized on it to advance his political career.

7. In 1950, McCarthy announced that he had a list of Communists who held positions in the U.S. State Department.

8. Correct

9. Eventually, more than 150 film workers, including performers, directors, and writers, were blacklisted by the Hollywood studios.

10. For the first half of the 1950s, anti-Communist leaders were very powerful in the United States; however, by 1955 McCarthy was in disgrace, and in 1957 the courts determined that membership in the Communist Party should no longer be a criminal offense in this country.

### Exercise 14.1 Answers (page 58)

1. In 1910, Robert Falcon Scott led his second expedition to Antarctica with two objectives: to collect scientific data and to be the first humans at the South Pole.

2. The years before World War I were a heady time for exploration of the frozen Antarctic continent.

3. The story of Scott's difficult journey continues to fascinate armchair adventurers even though the expedition was, in many ways, a failure.

4. After arriving in Antarctica, Scott's scientists began their work: they collected specimens, surveyed the land, and recorded twelve volumes of data.

5. Correct

6. Scott stuck to his original timetable for the South Pole journey: he did not want to engage in a race.

7. Scott and his men set out for the South Pole in the Antarctic summer of 1911, which is the winter season in the Northern Hemisphere.

8. Correct

9. As they traveled back to their base camp, death took all five men: Scott, Titus Oates, Edgar Evans, Henry Bowers, and Edward Wilson.

10. Correct

### Exercise 15.1 Answers (page 59)

1. The film producer shouted excitedly, "Everyone loves Shakespeare because he used so many familiar quotations!"

2. "When we make movies based on Shakespeare plays," he added, "we don't have to pay royalties to the writer."

3. Films based on Shakespeare plays try to reveal the relevance of his work to a modern audience.

4. Although Shakespeare lived four hundred years ago, his work is currently in demand in Hollywood.

5. *O, 10 things I Hate About You,* and *She's the Man* are just a few of Hollywood's modern interpretations of Shakespeare's plays.

6. The producer commented, "When I hear that a new film will be based on Shakespeare, I wonder, like Juliet, 'What's in a name?'"

7. If the name "Shakespeare" were not involved, would filmmakers be as interested in the material?

8. Shakespeare's plays are frequently performed in theaters, too, and several young playwrights recently wrote works based on his sonnets.

9. Hamlet, perhaps Shakespeare's most famous character, laments "Alas, poor Yorick! I knew him, Horatio, a fellow of infinite jest, of most excellent fancy."

10. Othello, one of Shakespeare's most complex characters, laments that he "loved not wisely, but too well."

## Exercise 16.1 Answers (page 60)

1. Correct

2. "[A]ll men are . . . endowed by their creator with certain inalienable rights, . . . among these are life, liberty, and the pursuit of happiness."

3. ". . . Thomas Jefferson wanted the Declaration of Independence to say that all men were 'created independent.'"

4. Elizabeth Cady Stanton's "Declaration of Sentiments" announces, "[W]e anticipate no small amount of misconception, misrepresentation, and ridicule. . . ."

5. "Stanton's 'Declaration of Sentiments' was based . . . on the language Jefferson had used in the Declaration of Independence."

6. Correct

7. "Allusions to the language of familiar literature . . . can lend authority to a text that uses them well."

8. Lincoln went on, "Fondly do we hope . . . that this mighty scourge of war may speedily pass away."

9. Martin Luther King Jr. expressed the wish that his children would be judged "by the content of their character."

10. "Repetition of structure can be an effective rhetorical device."

## Exercise 17.1 Answers (page 61)

1. African **chiefs'** stories led a German explorer to the stone ruins in Mashonaland, now in Zimbabwe, in 1871.

2. The explorer, **whose** name was Karl Mauch, tried to find out who had built the once great city.

3. The tribes nearby could not answer **Mauch's** question, but they knew gold had been found there.

4. The **Africans** called the site *Zimbabwe*.

5. Correct

6. He thought perhaps the **city's** builder was the Queen of Sheba.

7. An **archeologist's** findings later demonstrated that the city was about six hundred years old and that it had been built by African natives.

8. The Shona tribe probably built the first walls on the site, but **its** more complex structures were added later by the Rozwi tribe.

9. The Rozwi probably erected the temple, which was inhabited by Rozwi ruler-priests until their empire's end in the **1830s**.

10. The legends about the origins of the city persisted for a long time, perhaps because of white South **Africans'** and Europeans' resistance to the idea that black Africans had built the impressive structures.

### Exercise 18.1 Answers (page 62)

1. Bad movies (some of which are quite enjoyable to watch) often have a cult following.
2. Some films routinely make every critic's list of worst films (usually, these movies are so bad they are funny).
3. A few filmmakers (like Ed Wood) and movie companies (like American International Pictures) have acquired fame among fans of bad movies.
4. Roger Corman's American International Pictures (AIP) churned out innumerable inexpensive, quickly made films.
5. One Corman film, *Little Shop of Horrors* (1960), was filmed in less than three days.
6. But the director Edward D. Wood Jr. (1924–1978) has a special place in the world of bad movies.
7. Wood gained new fame with Tim Burton's film biography, *Ed Wood* (1994).
8. Like Corman's movies, Wood's were made very quickly, but Wood (unlike Corman) thought he was making great films.
9. Wood's "masterpiece," *Plan 9 from Outer Space* (Bela Lugosi's last film), is a science fiction and horror film with bad acting, dreadful writing, and laughable special effects.
10. Wood said that "*Plan 9* [was his] pride and joy."

### Exercise 19.1 Possible Answers (page 63)

1. Songbirds are a part of our national heritage—each state has its own official bird.
2. Some states have official birds unique to the region.
3. The nene—Hawaii's state bird—is a goose found only on those islands.
4. In Salt Lake City, a statue of a seagull, which is Utah's state bird, honors the birds that ate a huge swarm of locusts—without the birds, most crops would have been eaten by the insects.
5. Other states share popular state birds—the cardinal, the meadowlark, and the mockingbird are all official birds in at least five states.
6. When Americans think of spring, they often think of songbirds chirping in the trees.
7. For many years, the Audubon Society—an organization devoted to nature study—has studied populations of songbirds.
8. Birdwatchers—mainly trained volunteers—count birds in small local areas during the year-end holiday season.
9. The numbers of some songbirds—though fortunately not all—have declined alarmingly.
10. Although most people appreciate the sights and sounds of songbirds, they may not realize how modern human habits interfere with many birds' lives.

### Exercise 20.1 Answers (page 64)

1. At the turn of a new century and a new **millennium**, many people reflected on historical changes that had taken place in the previous hundred years.
2. In the late 1990s, Americans began making lists reflecting their choices of the greatest **events**, **literature**, people, and **films** of the century.

3. Most Americans would agree that the two **world wars** shaped the twentieth century and this country's role in it.

4. List makers might, however, dispute the importance of *Ulysses* or *Gone with the* ***Wind***.

5. Between the beginning and the end of the twentieth century, the United States changed from a minor player in global politics into the single undisputed **world power**.

6. Technology also advanced dramatically in the century of television, the *Apollo* space missions, and personal computers.

7. Of course, technology was sometimes used for evil purposes, as the **Holocaust** and nuclear weapons proved.

8. Some people would even argue that a significant development of the century was an increasing concern for the environment — **in** the United States, in Europe, and in parts of the **former** Soviet Union, among other places.

9. The trend toward urbanization saw people moving from rural areas to cities, with the result in this country that the **Great Plains** grew emptier while the **coasts**' population increased.

10. Only historical distance will reveal whether the twentieth century was "**the** best of times" or "**the** worst of times."

## Exercise 21.1 Answers (page 65)

1. When disasters strike, victims count on international organizations like the Red Cross and Doctors without Borders.

2. A **doctor's** help is often the most desperately needed form of aid.

3. People often offer canned goods and blankets, while major **corporations** receive tax benefits for donations of drugs and other medical supplies.

4. When Hurricane Mitch devastated Honduras, many U.S. **citizens** were quick to help.

5. A **registered nurse** who is willing to travel to the disaster area can provide needed services.

6. For several years, volunteer doctors have tried to alleviate the AIDS crisis in Africa.

7. In some situations, **such as** during outbreaks of deadly diseases or in war-torn areas, medical personnel risk their own lives.

8. Doctors from the Centers for Disease Control **(CDC) in Atlanta, Georgia**, travel the globe to isolate and study dangerous viruses.

9. The CDC doctors do not provide medical assistance in war zones, but other **organizations** do.

10. In the aftermath of bloody fighting, a U.N. peacekeeping force may arrive to find **international** doctors already at work.

## Exercise 22.1 Answers (page 66)

1. John Lennon, Paul McCartney, George Harrison, and Ringo Starr were **four** young men from Liverpool, England, who formed what would become the most popular rock band of all time.

2. On January **25**, 1964, the Beatles' first hit entered the U.S. charts.

3. The song "I Want to Hold Your Hand" spent seven weeks at number one and **four-teen** weeks in the top **forty**.

4. Almost immediately, the Beatles began to attract **thousands** of screaming fans everywhere they went.

5. Throughout the **1960s**, the Beatles were the world's most popular group.

6. During the eight years of the Beatles' reign on the charts, they had more than forty **3**-minute pop hits.

7. By the **second** half of the decade, the Beatles had stopped touring.

8. They performed live together for the last time on the roof of **3** Savile Row, the headquarters of their doomed record company, Apple.

9. **One hundred fifty** employees worked for Apple, which eventually went bankrupt.

10. By no means did each Beatle earn **25** percent of the group's profits, for Lennon and McCartney wrote more than **90** percent of the songs.

## Exercise 23.1 Answers (page 67)

1. Americans today get their information from *60 Minutes,* the *New York Times,* electronic sources, and thousands of other places.

2. Once, choices were limited: to find out about raising a child, for example, parents consulted Dr. Spock's book *Baby and Child Care.*

3. Now, magazines like *Parenting* compete with the new edition of Dr. Spock and dozens of other titles.

4. Obscure information is more accessible than ever, so a fan of the song "Telstar" can find *The Joe Meek Story,* a full-length biography of its producer.

5. A student wanting to learn about the dead language called Old English could consult Web sites like the one maintained by Georgetown University.

6. It may no longer be possible for a single person to know all about, for example, biology.

7. Once, the term *Renaissance man* or *Renaissance woman* referred to a person well educated and talented in many subjects.

8. Leonardo da Vinci, the original Renaissance man, not only painted the *Mona Lisa* but also wrote botanical treatises and devised remarkable engineering plans.

9. Today, we do not expect the builder of the ocean liner *Queen Elizabeth II* to know other subjects.

10. A lifetime of study may lie behind a single article in the *New England Journal of Medicine.*

## Exercise 24.1 Answers (page 68)

1. Does buying lottery tickets and entering sweepstakes make a person self-employed?

2. The odds of winning a major lottery prize are often over a million to one.

3. Yet many people, including desperately poor ones who cannot afford the tickets, buy large numbers of them when the jackpot is high and the odds are worst.

4. A sensible approach to such sky-high odds would be not to enter the lottery at all.

5. Sweepstakes are well known to anyone with a mailbox.

6. Unlike lotteries, apparently free sweepstakes do not require any cash investment other than the price of a stamp.

7. Yet many sweepstakes imply that buying a magazine subscription or a product improves the chances of winning.

8. Some sweepstakes companies have been accused of trying to dupe customers who do not read the fine print.

9. Some elderly people have thrown away their great-grandchildren's inheritance, buying hundreds of products they don't need from sweepstakes advertisers.

10. The idea of getting rich with minimal work or investment is so strikingly attractive that many people put logic aside and come up with the money.

## Exercise 25.1  Answers (page 69)

Focus groups consist of people selected to express **their** opinions about products **ranging** from sneakers and gum to movies. **Sometimes** people who are supposed to be experts on a subject are selected. When **companies** test a new product, they choose people who might **realistically** be expected to **buy** it. If marketers are **trying** out a new soft drink, for example, they might ask **teenagers** for their **advice**. A company **making** a **luxury** car would be more inclined to seek the **views** of upper-middle-class buyers. On other **occasions**, a focus group is picked at **random**. To find out how much **consumers** like a new TV show, a network might ask shoppers at a mall to watch an episode and discuss it with other **participants**. The network could **then** learn, not only what viewers like and dislike about the show, but also which groups are most **likely** to watch it. This information helps the network determine what changes to make in the show and what **sponsors** to approach. Of course, **since** many people **prefer** the familiar, focus groups sometimes **ensure** that **tried** and true formulas **occur** again and again at the expense of new ideas.

## Exercise 26.1  Answers (page 70)

1. The first American land set aside for a national public park was Yellowstone National Park, which was established in 1872 by President Ulysses S. Grant.

2. Yellowstone National Park has not only beautiful scenery but also the strange results of ancient volcanoes.

3. Underground lava left from millions of years ago heats cold groundwater.

4. This heating results in hot springs, geysers, and boiling **mud**.

5. Sequoia National Park, **the** second national park established in the United States, is the home of many giant sequoia trees.

6. To the north of Sequoia National Park is the third oldest national park, Yosemite National Park.

7. Like Sequoia National Park, Yosemite National Park offers **an** area of incredible beauty.

8. **Waterfalls** are found in some of our nation's oldest parks, such as Yosemite National Park and Niagara Reservation State Park.

9. Many other national parks have unusual natural formations; Denali National Park, for example, contains **the** highest mountain in North America.

10. A visitor who takes the time to see America's national parks will have **an** experience he or she will never forget.

**Exercise 26.2  Answers** (page 71)

1. shrimp
2. cream
3. beds
4. furniture
5. smoke
6. books
7. sand
8. tools
9. equipment
10. mail

**Exercise 27.1  Answers** (page 72)

1. to play
2. playing
3. took
4. moved
5. had formed
6. began
7. was
8. to play
9. had just turned
10. Correct

**Exercise 27.2  Answers** (page 73)

1. to work
2. sharing
3. to collaborate
4. plagiarizing
5. cheating
6. to do
7. to judge
8. working
9. asking
10. angering

**Exercise 27.3 Answers** (page 74)

1. might
2. ought to
3. should
4. would
5. should
6. must
7. would
8. could
9. can
10. might

**Exercise 28.1 Answers** (page 75)

1. in
2. At
3. at
4. on
5. in
6. in
7. on
8. on
9. at
10. In

**Exercise 29.1 Answers** (page 76)

1. The first three quilts that I made were not very intricate.
2. Correct
3. Correct
4. The article said that the best memory quilts don't have new fabric in them.
5. To make the squares for my memory quilt, I cut up my son's old shirts and boxer shorts.
6. Correct
7. Assembling a memory quilt from these items was a good opportunity for me to make space in his bureau and to practice my sewing.
8. It was also a good opportunity for me to preserve his childhood memories.
9. Correct
10. He thought the quilt was a wonderful idea, and he now wants me to make a bigger one.

**Exercise 30.1 Possible Answers** (page 77)

1. Many people once believed that the twentieth century would produce medical miracles that would bring an end to infectious diseases.
2. At the end of the twentieth century, medical research had not made this wish a reality.
3. Vaccines removed some terrible illnesses, such as polio, from the list of childhood diseases.
4. One dangerous disease that completely disappeared in the twentieth century was smallpox.
5. However, a few laboratories can still provide access to samples of the virus to trusted researchers.
6. Ordinary people forgot their fears about smallpox, but other diseases soon took its place.
7. The AIDS epidemic struck many previously healthy young people in the 1980s.
8. AIDS proved that medical science could never declare total victory over disease.
9. In the same decade, other terrifying new viruses whose existence was until recently unknown, such as Ebola, raced through local populations.
10. Medicine today can reveal much more about diseases than people knew during medieval plagues, but this knowledge cannot always save the lives of sick people.

**Exercise 30.2 Answers** (page 78)

1. Speed limits are not a good idea.
2. Hector does not know the baseball scores.
3. He is not a baseball fan.
4. Olga does not understand the importance of math class.
5. Medical careers are not where math skills make the most difference.
6. Conversation is not acceptable in the library.
7. Morning is not the hardest time for Julia to concentrate.
8. Young hunters cannot shoot safely.
9. Marco never worries about the health of his relatives in Brazil.
10. The high school may not build a new gymnasium.

# Appendix

## *Writing Assessment*

The two assessment tests in this appendix will help you and your instructor determine aspects of your writing that you need to improve. The first test (pp. 107–108) assesses your ability to develop and support ideas about a topic and express them clearly and correctly in an essay. The second test (pp. 108–115) measures your ability to recognize and correct errors in grammar, punctuation, and mechanics.

## WRITING ASSESSMENT: WRITING ESSAYS

Choose *either* Essay Assignment A or Essay Assignment B for this writing assessment test. Although the essay assignments are from courses in interpersonal communications and sociology, you do not need any background in these subject areas to write either essay. For whichever option you choose, then, draw from your personal experience for ideas for the essay. Be sure your essay is about the topic you choose and that it states, develops, and supports one main point about your topic. When you have finished drafting your essay, be sure to revise, edit, and proofread it. Your instructor will evaluate your final essay and identify any writing skills that need improvement. With your instructor's feedback, you will then be able to use the Action Plan Checklist (p. 116) to find help with those skills that need improvement.

### Essay Assignment A

Suppose you are taking a course in interpersonal communications and have been assigned a two-page essay on one of the following topics. Choose a topic, develop a thesis statement, and support your thesis with evidence.

1. Describe a communication breakdown you have observed or experienced, telling what happened, why it happened, and what could have been done to prevent it.

2. Pretend that you are preparing for a job interview. Describe the communication and leadership skills you would bring to the position of assistant manager at a department store.

3. Recall a conflict, disagreement, or argument you have had with someone. What feelings and emotions did you and the other person express? Explain how you communicated those feelings to each other and how the conflict was (or was not) resolved.

4. Explain how you can tell when a person doesn't mean what he or she says, using people you know as examples.

## Essay Assignment B

Suppose you are taking a sociology course and have been assigned a two-page essay on *one* of the following topics. Choose a topic, develop a thesis statement, and support your thesis with evidence.

1. Describe one important function of the family in American life. Explain why it is important and what is expected of family members. Use your own family as an example.

2. Explain one important function of dating in the United States. Support your ideas with your own dating experiences.

3. Examine one major function of the wedding ceremony. Why is this function important? Use weddings that you have attended or been involved in as evidence to support your thesis.

## WRITING ASSESSMENT: RECOGNIZING AND CORRECTING SENTENCE ERRORS

Most of the following sentences contain errors; some are correct as written. Look in the <u>underlined</u> part of each sentence for errors in usage, punctuation, grammar, capitalization, or sentence construction. Then choose the one revision that corrects the sentence error(s). If the original sentence contains no errors, select "d. no change." Circle the letter of the item you choose as your answer. An interactive version of this assessment is available by visiting the student site for *Successful College Writing* at www.bedfordstmartins.com/successfulcollege and clicking on *Exercise Central*.

1. <u>Lonnie and Robert should put his ideas together</u> and come up with a plan of action for the class project.

    a. Lonnie and Robert should put his idea together
    b. Lonnie and Robert should put her ideas together
    c. Lonnie and Robert should put their ideas together
    d. no change

2. The school district newsletter informs <u>all parents of beneficial programs for you and your children</u>.

    a. all parents of beneficial programs for your children.
    b. each parent about beneficial programs for you and your children.
    c. you of all beneficial programs for you and your children.
    d. no change

3. Margaret earned an A <u>on her term paper, consequently, she</u> was excused from taking the final exam.

    a. on her term paper; consequently, she
    b. on her term paper, consequently; she
    c. on her term paper consequently, she
    d. no change

4. Some students choose courses <u>without studying degree requirements these students often make</u> unwise choices.

    a. without studying degree requirements, these students often make
    b. without studying degree requirements. These students often make
    c. without studying degree requirements; so these students often make
    d. no change

5. Twenty-five band members <u>picked up their instruments from their chairs which were tuned and began to play</u>.

    a. picked up their tuned instruments from their chairs and began to play.
    b. picked up their instruments from their chairs tuned and began to play.
    c. picked up and began to play their instruments from their chairs which were tuned.
    d. no change

6. I am sure I <u>did good on my midterm exam</u> because it seemed easy to me.

    a. did awful good on my midterm exam
    b. did real good on my midterm exam
    c. did well on my midterm exam
    d. no change

7. In many American families, the financial decisions are made jointly by <u>husband and wife, the wife</u> makes most of the routine household decisions.

    a. husband and wife, in contrast the wife
    b. husband and wife the wife
    c. husband and wife. The wife
    d. no change

8. Professor Simmons <u>pace while he lectures</u>.

    a. pacing while he lectures.
    b. pace while he lecture.
    c. paces while he lectures.
    d. no change

9. When Tara set <u>the cup on the glass-topped table, it broke</u>.

    a. her cup on the glass-topped table, she broke it.
    b. the cup on the table with a glass top; it broke.
    c. it on the glass-topped table, the cup broke.
    d. no change

10. <u>Swimming to shore, my arms got tired</u>.

    a. My arms got tired swimming to shore.
    b. When I was swimming to shore, my arms got tired.
    c. My arms, swimming to shore, got tired.
    d. no change

11. Thousands of fans waited <u>to get into the stadium. Swarmed around the parking lot</u> like angry bees until security opened the gates.

    a. to get into the stadium. Swarming around the parking lot
    b. to get into the stadium; swarmed around the parking lot
    c. to get into the stadium. They swarmed around the parking lot
    d. no change

12. <u>After I left the college library I went</u> to the computer lab.

    a. After I left the college library, I went
    b. After leaving the college library I went
    c. After I left the college library; I went
    d. no change

13. <u>To be honest is better than dishonesty</u>.

    a. Being honest is better than dishonesty.
    b. To be honest is better than being dishonest.
    c. It is better to be honest than dishonest.
    d. no change

14. The amount of time <u>students spend researching a topic depends on his familiarity</u> with the topic.

    a. students spend researching a topic depends on his or her familiarity

    b. students spend researching a topic depends on their familiarity

    c. a student spends researching a topic depends on their familiarity

    d. no change

15. After Carlos completed <u>his term paper, he seems</u> less tense.

    a. his term paper, he seemed

    b. his term paper, he will seem

    c. his term paper, he is seeming

    d. no change

16. <u>When Maria tried to sign up for those courses in the fall, but they were full</u>.

    a. When Maria tried to sign up for those courses in the fall; however, they were full.

    b. Although Maria tried to sign up for those courses in the fall, but they were full.

    c. Maria tried to sign up for those courses in the fall, but they were full.

    d. no change

17. A course in nutrition <u>may be useful; it may help you make</u> wise food choices.

    a. may be useful, it may help you make

    b. may be useful it may help you make

    c. may be useful; because it may help you make

    d. no change

18. According to the reporter, <u>many pets are run over by automobiles roaming around untended</u>.

    a. many pets are run over roaming around untended by automobiles.

    b. many pets roaming around untended are run over by automobiles.

    c. many pets who are run over by automobiles roaming around untended.

    d. no change

19. You need to take <u>life more serious if you hope to do well</u> in school.

    a. life more serious if you hope to do good

    b. life more seriously if you hope to do well

    c. life seriouser if you hope to do well

    d. no change

20. Leon has already taken <u>three social sciences courses, Introduction to Psychology</u>, Sociology 201, and Anthropology 103.

    a. three social sciences courses; Introduction to Psychology,

    b. three social sciences courses: Introduction to Psychology,

    c. three social sciences courses. Introduction to Psychology,

    d. no change

21. <u>There's several people who can</u> advise you about the engineering program.

    a. There are several people who can
    b. There is several people who can
    c. There's two people who can
    d. no change

22. <u>In Chapter 6 of your book it describes</u> the causes of mental illness.

    a. In Chapter 6 of your book, they describe
    b. Chapter 6 of your book describes
    c. In Chapter 6 of the book, it describes
    d. no change

23. <u>Flood damage was visible crossing the river.</u>

    a. Flood damage was visible, crossing the river.
    b. Crossing the river, the flood damage was visible.
    c. Flood damage was visible as we crossed the river.
    d. no change

24. She had to leave the <u>van in the driveway. The heavy, wet snow halfway up</u> the garage door.

    a. van in the driveway. The heavy, wet snow had piled halfway up
    b. van in the driveway. Because of the heavy, wet snow halfway up
    c. van in the driveway; the heavy, wet snow halfway up
    d. no change

25. Mail <u>carriers who have been bitten by dogs are</u> wary of them.

    a. carriers, who have been bitten by dogs, are
    b. carriers who have been bitten, by dogs, are
    c. carriers who, having been bitten by dogs, are
    d. no change

26. Alfonso <u>need to practice</u> his clarinet every day.

    a. needing to practice
    b. needes to practice
    c. needs to practice
    d. no change

27. <u>Everyone should be sure to bring their notebook</u> to class on Wednesday.

    a. Everyone should be sure to bring their notebooks
    b. Everyone should be sure to bring his or her notebook
    c. Everyone should be sure to bring his notebook
    d. no change

28. <u>The television program ended Janelle read a book</u> to her son.

    a. When the television program ended, Janelle read a book
    b. The television program ended and Janelle read a book

c. The television program ended, Janelle read a book
d. no change

29. Georgia <u>replied "The way to a man's heart is through his stomach."</u>

a. replied "The way to a man's heart is through his stomach".
b. replied; "The way to a man's heart is through his stomach."
c. replied, "The way to a man's heart is through his stomach."
d. no change

30. The <u>plan to travel to three cities in two days seem</u> overly ambitious.

a. plan to travel to three cities in two days are
b. plan to travel to three cities in two days seems
c. plan to travel to three cities in two days do seem
d. no change

31. <u>You discover that your concentration improves</u> with practice, so now I can study more in less time.

a. I discovered that my concentration improves
b. You discover that concentration improves
c. You discovered that your concentration improves
d. no change

32. I couldn't watch the <u>rest of the football game. Because there was no chance that we could win</u> now. We were behind by three touchdowns.

a. rest of the football game and there was no chance that we could win
b. rest of the football game because there was no chance that we could win
c. rest of the football game; because there was no chance that we could win
d. no change

33. <u>"Shopping" Barbara explained "is</u> a form of relaxation for me."

a. "Shopping" Barbara explained, "is
b. "Shopping," Barbara explained "is
c. "Shopping," Barbara explained, "is
d. no change

34. <u>A balanced diet, exercising regularly, and to get enough sleep</u> are essential to good health.

a. Eating a balanced diet, exercising regularly, and to get enough sleep
b. A balanced diet, regular exercise, and enough sleep
c. To eat a balanced diet, exercising regularly, and to get enough sleep
d. no change

35. <u>The use of air bags was designed</u> to increase driver and passenger safety.

a. Air bags were designed
b. The use of air bags were designed

    c. Increased use of air bags was designed

    d. no change

36. The <u>articles and the book contains</u> the information I need.

    a. book and the articles contains

    b. articles and the book contain

    c. articles and the book has contained

    d. no change

37. Top firms are always <u>looking for skilled managers. People who can adapt</u> to changing times and rise to new challenges.

    a. looking for skilled managers; people who can adapt

    b. looking for skilled managers. People, who can adapt

    c. looking for skilled managers who can adapt

    d. no change

38. <u>Individuals and community groups can assist students in financial need, and</u> help them secure a good education.

    a. Individuals and community groups, can assist students in financial need and

    b. Individuals, and community groups can assist students in financial need, and

    c. Individuals and community groups can assist students in financial need and

    d. no change

39. <u>Someone left their briefcase</u> under the table.

    a. Everyone left their briefcase

    b. Someone left their briefcases

    c. Someone left his or her briefcase

    d. no change

40. Mustard is a versatile <u>seasoning and it can be</u> used to enhance the flavor of many dishes.

    a. seasoning; and it can be

    b. seasoning, and it can be

    c. seasoning, therefore it can be

    d. no change

41. We spent our most happiest days in the little cottage on the lake.

    a. spent our happiest days

    b. spent our more happiest days

    c. spent our more happy days

    d. no change

42. Swimming is an <u>excellent form of exercise, it produces</u> a good aerobic workout.

    a. excellent form of exercise it produces

    b. excellent form of exercise and it produces

c. excellent form of exercise because it produces
d. no change

For a guide to scoring your assessment, turn to p. 117.

## ACTION PLAN CHECKLIST

The Action Plan Checklist on the next page will help you find the appropriate resources for improving the writing skills that you and your instructor have identified as problem areas.

### Resources

1. **Part 7: Handbook: Writing Problems and How to Correct Them.** The Handbook section of *Successful College Writing* contains a systematic review of the rules that correspond to most of the topics listed under "Sentence Skills" in the Action Plan Checklist, as well as exercises to help you understand and apply the rules.

2. *Exercise Central* **and** *Additional Exercises for Successful College Writing.* The exercises in the workbook and online at **http://bcs.bedfordstmartins.com /exercisecentral/Home.aspx** offer you practice in applying the principles presented in Part 7. The workbook and *Exercise Central* contain additional exercises for all the topics listed in the Action Plan Checklist as well as other topics you may wish to review. These resources are designed so that you can check your answers immediately after completing an exercise. As you work through each exercise, be sure to take the time to discover why you answered any items incorrectly and, if you are still uncertain, to check with a classmate or your instructor.

3. Writing Guide Software for ***Successful College Writing.*** This interactive computer program provides a comprehensive review of many of the topics included in the Action Plan Checklist as well as other key topics. The software includes a tutorial for most of the problem areas identified under "Sentence Skills."

For more practice with the sentence skills listed in the table on the next page, go to **www.bedfordstmartins.com/successfulcollege** for the *Exercise Central* Study Plan for *Successful College Writing* and click the link to *Exercise Central*. Click the arrow next to "Handbook" on the left-hand side of the page. Exercises for all of the sentence skills listed in the table on page 116 can be found by clicking the arrows next to "Writing Correct Sentences," "Using Punctuation Correctly," and "Managing Mechanics and Spelling."

**ACTION PLAN CHECKLIST**
**Directions: Place a check mark next to each skill that you or your instructor has identified as a problem area.**

| Skills That Need Improvement | | Resources That Will Help You | |
|---|---|---|---|
| *Paragraph Skills* | ✓ | *Text/Handbook** | *Workbook* |
| Details–Relevant | | Ch. 8 | Exercise P.3 |
| Details–Specific | | Ch. 8 | Exercise P.5 |
| Topic Sentences | | Ch. 8 | Exercise P.1 |
| Topic Sentences | | Ch. 8 | Exercise P.2 |
| | | | |
| *Sentence Skills* | | | |
| Adjective and Adverb Usage | | H9 | Exercise 9.1 |
| Capitalization | | H20 | Exercise 20.1 |
| Colon Usage | | H14 | Exercise 14.1 |
| Comma Splices | | H4 | Exercise 4.1 |
| Comma Usage | | H12 | Exercise 12.1, 12.2 |
| Dangling Modifiers | | H10 | Exercise 10.1 |
| Sentence Fragments | | H3 | Exercise 3.1 |
| Misplaced Modifiers | | H10 | Exercise 10.1 |
| Mixed Constructions | | H8 | Exercise 8.2 |
| Parallelism | | Ch. 10 | Exercise E.4 |
| Pronoun-Antecedent Agreement | | H7 | Exercise 7.2 |
| Pronoun Reference | | H7 | Exercise 7.1 |
| Punctuation of Quotations | | H15 | Exercise 15.1 |
| Run-On Sentences | | H4 | Exercise 4.1 |
| Semicolon Usage | | H13 | Exercise 13.1 |
| Shifts | | H8 | Exercise 8.1 |
| Subject-Verb Agreement | | H5 | Exercise 5.1 |
| Spelling | | H25 | Exercise 25.1 |
| Verb Forms | | H6 | Exercise 6.1 |

*Handbook sections are preceded by the letter *H* in this chart.

## Working through Your Action Plan

Once you have filled in the check marks in your Action Plan Checklist, use the following suggestions to achieve maximum success in improving your writing skills.

1. Begin by reading the appropriate section(s) in Chapters 5 and 7 and in Part 7 and studying the examples. You may have to read the material several times to grasp it fully.

2. Test your understanding of a particular rule or explanation by looking away from the text and writing the rule or principle in your own words in your journal. If you cannot do so, you do not fully understand the rule. Try discussing

it with a classmate and your instructor and recording what you learn from them in your own words. When you can explain the principle or rule in your own words, you are more apt to understand and remember the material.

3. Once you are confident that you understand a rule or explanation for a sentence skill or problem, complete the corresponding exercise in the Handbook, the workbook, or online.

4. Set a deadline by which you will understand the rules and complete the exercises for all of your problem areas. Try to complete everything within the next two to three weeks. The sooner you understand this essential material, the sooner you will be fully prepared to write clear, effective essays.

## SCORING AND INTERPRETING YOUR GRAMMAR ASSESSMENT

Score your assessment by using the answer key that follows. Each question assesses your ability to recognize and correct a particular sentence problem. In the answer key, circle the number of each item you answered incorrectly.

### Answer Key: Error Correction Self-Assessment

| Answer | Sentence Skill or Problem |
|---|---|
| 1. c | Pronoun-Antecedent Agreement |
| 2. c | Shift in Person |
| 3. a | Comma Splice |
| 4. b | Run-On Sentence |
| 5. a | Misplaced Modifier |
| 6. c | Adverb and Adjective Usage |
| 7. c | Comma Splice |
| 8. c | Subject-Verb Agreement |
| 9. c | Pronoun Reference |
| 10. b | Dangling Modifier |
| 11. c | Sentence Fragment |
| 12. a | Comma Usage |
| 13. c | Parallelism |
| 14. b | Pronoun-Antecedent Agreement |
| 15. a | Shift in Tense |
| 16. c | Mixed Construction |
| 17. d | Semicolon Usage |
| 18. b | Misplaced Modifier |
| 19. b | Adverb and Adjective Usage |
| 20. b | Colon Usage |
| 21. a | Subject-Verb Agreement |

22. b          Pronoun Reference
23. c          Dangling Modifier
24. a          Sentence Fragment
25. d          Comma Usage
26. c          Verb Form
27. b          Pronoun-Antecedent Agreement
28. a          Run-On Sentence
29. c          Punctuation of Quotation
30. b          Subject-Verb Agreement
31. a          Shift in Point of View
32. b          Sentence Fragment
33. c          Comma Usage
34. b          Parallelism
35. a          Mixed Construction
36. b          Subject-Verb Agreement
37. c          Sentence Fragment
38. c          Comma Usage
39. c          Pronoun-Antecedent Agreement
40. b          Comma Usage
41. a          Adverb and Adjective Usage
42. c          Comma Splice